A COMPLETE GUIDE FOR SINGLE DADS:

Everything You Need to Know About Raising Healthy, Happy Children On Your Own

By Craig W. Baird

A COMPLETE GUIDE FOR SINGLE DADS: EVERYTHING YOU NEED TO KNOW ABOUT RAISING HEALTHY, HAPPY CHILDREN ON YOUR OWN

Library of Congress Cataloging-in-Publication Data

Baird, Craig W., 1980-
  A complete guide for single dads : everything you need to know about raising healthy, happy children on your own / by Craig W. Baird.
     p. cm.
  Includes bibliographical references and index.
  ISBN-13: 978-1-60138-396-9 (alk. paper)
  ISBN-10: 1-60138-396-7 (alk. paper)
  1. Single fathers. 2. Child rearing. 3. Parenting. I. Title.
  HQ759.915.B335 2010
  649'.10243--dc22
                        2009050683

PROJECT MANAGER: Kim Fulscher • EDITORIAL INTERN: Amy Gronauer
INTERIOR & COVER DESIGN: Jackie Miller • millerjackiej@gmail.com
PRE-PRESS & PRODUCTION DESIGN: Holly Marie Gibbs

Printed on Recycled Paper

Printed in the United States

We recently lost our beloved pet "Bear," who was not only our best and dearest friend but also the "Vice President of Sunshine" here at Atlantic Publishing. He did not receive a salary but worked tirelessly 24 hours a day to please his parents. Bear was a rescue dog that turned around and showered myself, my wife, Sherri, his grandparents  Jean, Bob, and Nancy, and every person and animal he met (maybe not rabbits) with friendship and love. He made a lot of people smile every day.

We wanted you to know that a portion of the profits of this book will be donated to The Humane Society of the United States. *–Douglas & Sherri Brown*

The human-animal bond is as old as human history. We cherish our animal companions for their unconditional affection and acceptance. We feel a thrill when we glimpse wild creatures in their natural habitat or in our own backyard.

Unfortunately, the human-animal bond has at times been weakened. Humans have exploited some animal species to the point of extinction.

The Humane Society of the United States makes a difference in the lives of animals here at home and worldwide. The HSUS is dedicated to creating a world where our relationship with animals is guided by compassion. We seek a truly humane society in which animals are respected for their intrinsic value, and where the human-animal bond is strong.

Want to help animals? We have plenty of suggestions. Adopt a pet from a local shelter, join The Humane Society and be a part of our work to help companion animals and wildlife. You will be funding our educational, legislative, investigative and outreach projects in the U.S. and across the globe.

Or perhaps you'd like to make a memorial donation in honor of a pet, friend or relative? You can through our Kindred Spirits program. And if you'd like to contribute in a more structured way, our Planned Giving Office has suggestions about estate planning, annuities, and even gifts of stock that avoid capital gains taxes.

Maybe you have land that you would like to preserve as a lasting habitat for wildlife. Our Wildlife Land Trust can help you. Perhaps the land you want to share is a backyard— that's enough. Our Urban Wildlife Sanctuary Program will show you how to create a habitat for your wild neighbors.

So you see, it's easy to help animals. And The HSUS is here to help.

THE HUMANE SOCIETY
OF THE UNITED STATES.

2100 L Street NW • Washington, DC 20037 • 202-452-1100
www.hsus.org

Dedication

To my wife and love, Layla.

Table of Contents

CHAPTER 2: HELPING THE KIDS COPE 53

CHAPTER 3: WORKING WITH YOUR EX-SPOUSE 69

CHAPTER 4: WIDOWHOOD 83

CHAPTER 6: CHILD CARE   125

CHAPTER 7: MANAGING STRESS   149

SECTION 3: THE ROLES OF THE FATHER   177

CHAPTER 8: DOCTOR   179

CHAPTER 9: COOK   205

Foreword

In 1996, my "feat of feet" — running almost 2,100 miles from Minneapolis to Atlanta at the Summer Olympics of Atlanta's opening ceremonies — was thought to be an impossible trek. I was told by doctors and seasoned runners that it was truly impossible to accomplish. Nevertheless, my goal was to run the equivalent of a marathon each day for 75 consecutive days to honor single parents and their kids. I was 57 years old and had never run more than a 10K in my life, but that did not stop me. I trained for 17 months, and many times went home at night to cough up blood while my body tried to make the pain stop. Halfway through my training, I had a heart attack, but returned to my training three weeks later.

I decided to complete this enormous task and write a book about it after my beautiful wife, Sue, passed away from breast cancer in her mid-30s. After she passed, I knew I would need help — for the emotional pain and for simple hugs. I knew it would be very hard. All I knew was work — I did not know how to cook meals or know how to shop for my kids' clothes. This book — Craig Baird's *A Complete Guide for Single Dads: Everything you Need to Know About Raising Healthy, Happy Children On Your Own* — will teach you all of that, so you won't have to fumble as I did.

I was raised by grandparents who told me every day that nothing in life is impossible. Running to Atlanta was sort of like running home. Two of my three children were born in Atlanta, I worked for The Coca-Cola Company for eight years at its corporate offices, and to me the Olympics meant anything could be made possible. You must have faith to be able to accomplish what I did, but the mental part was also tough and could have easily destroyed my thinking, had it not been for my personal faith in God.

Baird's book comes at an opportune time — fathers need advice, help, and support. It is not easy to be a single dad, whether through divorce or widowhood. This book will teach you about divorce law, finding an attorney for custody, cooking, disciplinarian techniques, and how to communicate with your kids. You will learn how to raise kids whether you have support from an ex-spouse or not. Many single fathers also want to give back, tell their stories, and help others. This guide contains several stories from single fathers, along with tips from grief counselors and stories from children raised by single dads. I found that single fathers are, many times, lost in what to do and how to raise their kids. They need help, answers, and direction.

I certainly wish I had Baird's guide beside me on those many tough days and nights after my wife passed. It is a complete guide for all the many issues I faced, and then some. Every single father should read this many times over.

Terry Hitchcock
Single father and author of
A Father's Odyssey: 75 Marathons in 75 Consecutive Days
www.terryhitchcock.com

Introduction

Whether a man becomes a father as a result of divorce or death, there is always a difficult road ahead. Many fathers find the task of being a single parent overwhelming at first. They need to be a mother and a father, a cook and a friend, a disciplinarian and a teacher. There can be so much to learn and so much to know initially — many fathers wonder if they will get through it.

However, fathers do get through it and learn about their children, become a role model, and have relationships with their kids they never thought possible. It can be tough being a single father, but there have been many in the past who have done a good job. Single fathers need to find ways to adapt to their new circumstances, and they need to adapt fast. It can be hard when you wonder if you are doing a good job, but that is why there is help out there like this book. There are many organizations that help single fathers, to give them a firm foundation of understanding that will allow the fathers to raise their children in a proper manner.

Becoming a single father is something that changes your life completely. All the tasks that were once done together are now done by the father alone. It is a daunting change and a difficult thing to work through. Fathers can become a single parent through divorce or widowhood; both events are challenging, and more and more fathers are going through it. About 100,000 men a year become widowers. About half of all marriages in the United States end in divorce.

When children are involved, divorce is far from a simple matter. Fathers both need custody of their children and to have a relationship with them. However, custody courts usually favor mothers, leaving fathers with partial or no custody. Movements have been started, like the Fathers' Rights Movement, to help balance the custody playing field, but it can still be hard.

Single fathers often struggle in the beginning, but it forges a stronger bond with their children in the end. If a father loses his wife because of death, he will love his children that much more because they are his last link to his lost wife. If he loses his wife through divorce, he will love his children that much more because he wants to show them that no matter what happens, he is always there for them.

There is a lot to being a single father. Some of the hats you will wear include:

- Being a teacher and a role model by helping your children through their schooling.

- Being a disciplinarian by giving your children rules and boundaries that they need to follow.

- Being a cook and ensuring that your children eat right and lead healthy lives through the meals you make them.

- Being a friend to your children by playing with, encouraging, and bonding with them.

Fathers are the role models that children have. They allow children to see the world through their father's eyes from an early age. As a father, the example you set for your children is based on the actions you display in front of them. They say that a father is not a father simply because of the birth of a child: A father must earn the right to be called a father.

As a father, it is up to you to ensure that your children get a good foundation for their lives. You can teach them about being kind to others, respecting the rules, and being good sports through everything in life. As a single father, it can be hard to do these things, especially when it comes to discipline, but your children look up to you. Even in their teen years when they want nothing to do with you, your children will look at you and respect you.

There are many things that you have to think about when you are a single father. These include ways to keep your children busy, who is going to baby-sit the children when you are at work, when to have the sex talk with them, and what to do when they hit puberty. Puberty can be a trying time for a single father. You have to deal with issues that you may not want to talk about, or that you do not really know much about, especially with a daughter. However, this is a unique time for your children and they need to know that what is happening to them is normal. You cannot rely on school to teach them the basics. They need to hear it from their father.

Beyond these trials and tribulations, being a father is an incredibly rewarding time of life. You will look back at being a single father and remember the great times you have had. There will be tough times and sad times, but overall the experience will leave you stronger and a better person for it. Years down the road, whether you are divorced or widowed, your children will look back on the time they spent with you as children of a single father and know you did your best in often trying circumstances.

You will find myriad resources in this book, such as cooking tips, information about bonding with your kids, how to handle stress, and how to handle discipline. Being a single father is a slippery slope, but this book will give you some traction to find your footing and raise children you can be proud of, and who will be proud of you.

1

Dealing With Divorce and Widowhood

"A divorce is like an amputation:
You survive it, but there is less of you."

— Margaret Atwood, author

1

Legal Issues in Divorce — Custody, Child Support, and More

> *"Divorce is one of the most financially traumatic things you can go through. Money spent on getting mad or getting even is money wasted."*
>
> — Richard Wagner, American economist

Divorce happens. In the United States alone, roughly 45 percent of all marriages will end in divorce. When children are involved, it can be much worse for everyone included in the process. As the child's father, it is important to be aware of how divorce will affect your life. Custody, lawyers, and child support may all become part of your life for a time. It is unfortunate, but it is something that needs to be dealt with.

TALKING ABOUT CUSTODY

When you and your spouse talk about custody, you should immediately work through any problems with visitation. Custody is a tricky subject for many fathers because of the large number who end up not getting custody of their children. Often, fathers will feel defensive and try to convince their ex-partners they should have joint custody. When you are going to talk about custody, you should not be aggressive or confrontational. Be level-headed when you talk to your ex-partner about custody, share your own concerns, and discuss what you hope to achieve. Having an agreement between you and your ex-partner can keep the children out of the court system. This is best for everyone, especially the children.

Be sure to listen to your ex-partner about what she wants out of custody and what kind of arrangement will work for her. Finding a balanced agreement saves you money on court costs, saves your children stress, and can help you develop a better relationship with your ex-partner.

THE COST OF CUSTODY

The Number 1 legal ramification of divorce that most fathers care about is not how much they pay in alimony, but how much time they will get to spend with their children. There are some surprising statistics from the Center for Children's Justice related to custody and divorced fathers in the United States:

- Roughly 37.9 percent of all fathers have no access or visitation rights to their children.

- Over one-third, 40 percent, of mothers have reported that they interfered with the visitation right of the father on at least one occasion to punish their ex-partner.

- More than half of all divorced mothers do not see the value in the father having contact with the children.

- Just over 10 percent of mothers want the opinion of their ex-partners when dealing with issues relating to parenting.

- For fathers, 70 percent feel they have too little time with their children on a regular basis.

As can be seen from these statistics, fathers do not always get the best deal when it comes to custody. While things are changing, usually the mother will receive more custody than the father. This is a shift from how custody was dealt with for much of history. Before the Twentieth Century, children were believed to be the property of the father. As a result of this, fathers almost always had custody over the mother in this unfair system. In the Twentieth Century, things began to change as courts started to award custody to mothers rather than fathers. According to the Divorce Lawyer Source Web site, roughly 70 percent of all custody cases award custody to the mother. Only 20 percent of all cases are joint custody and fathers who receive full custody represent less than 10 percent of all cases. This is an improvement though, because 40 percent of all child custody cases in 1991 gave no custody to the father at all, including any visitation rights. Divorce Lawyer Source may help you in finding updated custody law information for the state in which you live. The Web site also includes information about other divorce and family-related law. Visit their Web site at **www.divorce-lawyer-source.com.**

Financial cost to the father

Fighting for custody, even just joint custody, will cost you. This is especially true if there has already been a court battle for custody and you are attempting to gain more custody. Typically, most fathers will pay roughly $5,000 minimum to start a custody battle with their ex-partners. Rarely, if ever, does the financial cost of custody stay that low. Factoring in lawyer costs, travel costs, and court fees, many fathers will pay double to 10 times as much in their own battle for custody. Some fathers have even paid $100,000 or more in court costs for the privilege of seeing their children on a regular basis.

One important point to remember is that if a father loses custody, he can also be charged with paying for his ex-partner's attorney fees. This can drive up the cost of the court battle past $150,000. It is not unusual for a father to go bankrupt from the effort to see his children.

Emotional cost to the father

Far beyond the financial cost to the father is the emotional cost. For many fathers, it is stressful to deal with courts and the emotional impact that comes with being separated from their children. Many fathers fall into a deep depression because of the custody battle and the judgment by the courts. About 75 percent of divorced fathers said that missing their children was by far the worst part of the divorce, according to *Divorce: Causes and Consequences* by Alison Clark-Stewart and Cornelia Brentano. Also mentioned in the book was the fact that when a father does not get custody, he feels victimized, lost, and frustrated. Fathers without custody are at a higher risk for depression and substance abuse. Sadly, fathers who lose or have limited custody of their children are often more likely to commit suicide, as well.

This does not mean you will experience anything like this. It is possible to have a custody agreement that is fair and balanced, and there are many fathers who are happy with the arrangements the courts determine. Regardless of how the custody process goes, fathers will feel stressed and frustrated. They have little control over the custody process, and many will feel that their ability to be a father is constantly questioned. Fathers will feel scrutinized and interrogated at times. The important thing for any father to remember is that he needs to keep an eye on the goal of getting joint custody with his ex-partner.

HOW CUSTODY AFFECTS THE CHILDREN

Custody has a significant impact on children. According to Richard O'Connor, Ph.D. and author of *Undoing Depression: What Therapy Doesn't Teach You and Medication Can't Give You*, 45 percent of all children in the United States will go through and have to adjust to the divorce process. There are several other disturbing factors of how custody affects children and why it is so important for both parents to work together.

- On average, children from divorced families are twice as likely to have mental problems as children from intact families, according to O'Connor.

- Children of divorce are two to three times more likely to have emotional problems than children from intact families.

In Chapter 2, the issue of children feeling guilty over the divorce will be covered, but in regards to custody, children often feel frustrated that their parents are not together. They will also be stressed because they have to travel between households and may often feel as though they are caught in the middle of their parent's battle for their love and affection. The type of custody that you get will have a big effect on how you feel about yourself and about the entire custody process.

CASE STUDY: A FATHER'S CUSTODY BATTLE

Todd Palmer
Single father, Michigan

My custody battle lasted nearly two years, and it was pure hell. My ex-wife and her legal team dragged me through endless accusations of abuse of my son, court hearings, encounters with child protective services, three separate psychological evaluators, and eventually forced me to seek only supervised visitation for her once I did earn custody. The legal costs were in the neighborhood of $70,000, which put me into bankruptcy and caused me to lose my home and car. I ran out of money for attorneys and had to handle my own legal work for a period of three years after receiving custody. As far as I know, I was the first non-attorney to speak at my own state court of appeals hearing.

When I went through my custody battle in the early 1990s, it was the prevalent belief that mothers were the "better" parent, based on their gender. In Wayne County, where I had my custody battle, fathers received custody less than 1 percent of the time. I had to prove multiple times that I was the better parent.

Being a single dad was not a factor with the people in my life. They simply saw my son and I as a family and accepted us as they would any other family. The only time I remember it being an issue was when I went on a date and the young lady I was having dinner with asked me, "How could you take your son from his mother?" I was so offended at the statement, I became speechless.

The best part of being a single dad is being able to participate in watching my son grow up on a daily basis, including attending school functions, sporting activities, and eating dinner with him each night. Since I was a single parent when my son was younger than 2 years old, I did not have any previous co-parenting situation to compare it to. I never really wanted to be married again and was comfortable being on my own, solely raising my son.

TYPES OF CUSTODY

There are three primary forms of custody: sole parental responsibility, primary residential custody, and rotating/joint custody. Each type of custody creates different responsibilities for the parents and each has an emotional impact on the children.

Sole parental responsibility

With this type of custody, one parent has complete legal custody. This is used primarily when there is a history of sexual or physical abuse with the parent who does not receive custody, or if there is an alcohol or drug problem. The parent who has sole custody is the one who legally makes all the decisions concerning the children, including decisions regarding their welfare and how much time the children can spend with their other parent. With this type of custody, a court-appointed supervisor will supervise visitation with the other parent.

Primary residential custody

This is the form of custody used heavily before the mid-part of the Twentieth Century, in which the children share time between two households in an arrangement that is negotiated by the parents. If the parents cannot agree on a schedule, the judge will choose one. In this type of custody arrangement, the children spend more time in one home than the other. A typical arrangement will have the children spending every other weekend with the non-primary parent, and Wednesday evenings. Often, a week or two in the summer will also be spent with the non-primary parent.

Rotating custody

This is often called joint custody or shared physical custody. This is the most accepted and typical of the custody agreements in North America. It is often cited as the most successful as well, since both parents are working together, albeit separately, to raise the children. In this arrangement, the primary parent duties shift equally between parents, with no parent having more of a say over the welfare of the children than the other parent.

For this type of arrangement, both parents need to work together to ensure the best emotional well-being for the children. While many parents choose this arrangement, sometimes the courts decide this is the best custody agreement for the parents, and the parents are required to follow it.

Schedules for this can vary with each parent having the children on a revolving weekly basis. An example of this would be:

WEEK NUMBER	PARENT
1	Mother
2	Father
3	Mother
4	Father
5	Mother
6	Father

These three forms of custody are the most common, but there are some that are not used as often. These are systems that judges will sometimes choose because it is the best for the children. An important point to remember is that the judge is not going to choose what is best for the father or the mother, but what is best for the children. They are the innocent parties when it comes to divorce.

Divided/Alternating custody

With divided custody, or alternating custody, kids will switch back and forth between parents. The children will stay with each parent for about three to four months at a time. This is a very rare option because of the logistics of it, and it usually requires that each parent live relatively close to each other to make it easier on everyone. Parents need to live close together so the children are not going to new schools every few months.

Split custody

With split custody, if there is more than one child, each parent has custody of one or more children. For example, if there are four children, the mother would take two and the father would take two. If there are five children, one parent will have more children to care for. You will have visitation with the children who do not live with you based on a schedule your ex-partner creates, and likewise you will have control over their visitation with the children that live with you. This option should only be considered if it is absolutely the best idea for the children. Separating brothers and sisters can have a seriously detrimental effect on the children.

Bird's nest

A very rare option is the bird's nest option. With this custody arrangement, the children live in the same house, but the mother and father each take turns living in the house with the children, usually for a week at a time. This type of arrangement takes a great deal of compromise, rules, and cooperation between the mother and father to execute correctly. It should only be considered if the mother and father have the money to support such an arrangement. With this custody agreement, a mortgage needs to be paid on the house the kids live in, as well as mortgage/rent on the houses that the parents live in separately. This option is sometimes used after a split-up, when the house is on the market.

Serial custody

This type of custody is when the kids will live with a certain parent for a certain number of years before switching. This is not the best idea for a custody arrangement, but some parents choose it so that during the teenage years, the child will live with a same-sex parent. For example, the boy lives with his father, and the girl lives with her mother.

Third-party custody

This form of custody is when neither parent gets custody, and instead the child is put into the legal care of a grandparent or legal guardian. The parents then have visitation that is supervised by someone else, such as a court-appointed child advocate. This is often used when the judge rules that both the father and mother are unfit to raise the children properly, or if there is a history of physical, substance, or sexual abuse.

Sadly, some great fathers lose out on custody because their ex-partners may have excellent attorneys. To ensure you get a fair custody arrangement if you and your partner cannot agree on one, you will need a good attorney.

CHOOSING AN ATTORNEY

Having a good attorney in a custody battle is worth its weight in gold. There is a saying that having a good lawyer on your side is more important than having justice on your side. In some cases, it can be true. A good attorney can fight for you in court and help you get a fair settlement. Finding a good attorney who is affordable can be a bit more difficult to accomplish.

Finding the right attorney

There are several ways to go about finding a good attorney at an affordable price:

1. Talk to friends and family. Half of all marriages end in divorce, so if you have a large group of friends, some of them may have gone through a divorce. Talk with these friends and find out if they were happy with the divorce settlement and if they were happy with their lawyer. If they were, then you should get a referral to their lawyer.

2. If you already have a business lawyer at your disposal, then ask if he or she can provide you with a referral to good divorce lawyers.

3. Check out the local bar association, which will have a list of lawyers to choose from.

4. Go to a legal aid society. These lawyers will work cheaper than other lawyers and they are often quite skilled. This can be a great resource for a top-notch lawyer.

5. The American Bar Association's Web site, **www.abanet. org**, includes a lawyer referral system. Hover your cursor

over the "Public Resources" tab at the top of the Web page, and click the "Lawyer Locator" option. This will help you find a lawyer in your area, get free legal information, find out if a lawyer you have contacted is still licensed, and what to do if you are having problems with your lawyer. Click on the link for "Legal Information," and you will find another link for "ABA Divorce Information."

You should not choose the first lawyer you meet. Schedule consultations with two or three lawyers, or whatever your budget allows. Consultations can cost $100 to $800 per hour, depending on the lawyer. Choose the one who is right for you and can win what you want out of the divorce. Before you hire any lawyer, make sure you ask the right questions so there are no surprises down the road.

The questions to ask

Here is a quick list of some of the questions you should ask a prospective lawyer:

1. How long have you been practicing law?

2. How many years have you been a divorce lawyer?

3. What new laws may affect my case?

4. What is your payment and response policy on phone calls and e-mails?

5. Can you respond immediately to developments in the case and to my communications, within 24 hours?

6. Are you all right with the fact that my biggest concern is maintaining a cordial relationship with my ex-partner,

and ensuring my children are minimally impacted by the divorce?

7.   How much do you charge for each specific task that you will do, including document preparation, court appearances, and legal advice?

What to look for

Apart from the questions you should ask, there are certain things you should look for in your divorce lawyer:

- Always go with your instinct when you meet your lawyer. Does he or she listen to you? Do you feel comfortable with him or her? These are things you should look for when you talk to the lawyer.

- Do you feel that the lawyer has good negotiation skills?

- Is the attorney confrontational with you?

- Watch for whether or not the attorney returns calls to you quickly and on a regular basis. Does he or she share the overall plan with you, and does he or she communicate with clients on a regular basis?

- Does the attorney explain the divorce process to you so you know what you should expect and what will happen?

- Does the attorney allow clients to make the decisions by giving them enough information to make a proper decision?

- Do you find that the attorney works toward your goal of getting everything resolved in a proper manner?

- Is the attorney organized? Is his or her office a mess, or is everything in its place? An attorney who is organized is one who has a plan of action mapped out completely.

- Will the attorney allow you to take complete ownership of the case and let you know that the longer it drags on, the more it is going to cost?

A BRIEF UNDERSTANDING OF DIVORCE

There are two forms of divorce. There is the emotional divorce, which requires you to change the relationship you have with your ex-partner and your children because of different living arrangements and the change in the family dynamic. The second form is the legal divorce, which legally ends the marriage between you and your spouse.

Types of divorce

There are several different kinds of legal divorce that can be filed between you and your partner:

No-Fault Divorce

This is a divorce where no proof of fault by either partner is required. Some terms used in this type of divorce are incompatibility, breakdown of marriage, and irreconcilable differences. In Australia and Canada, a one-year separation is required before a divorce can proceed. In the United States, 49 states have a no-fault divorce law. New York is the only state that does not have no-fault divorce.

At-Fault Divorce

This is a divorce when something has happened, caused by one of the partners, to create the divorce. In the past, divorce was only granted on these grounds, but that has now changed. New York is the only state that now requires a fault in divorce. Adultery, abuse, or negligence in marriage are some of the many reasons for an at-fault divorce.

Summary Divorce

This is a rarer type of divorce, and it involves spouses meeting certain requirements to obtain the divorce. These factors can include:

- A marriage of less than five years
- No children
- No property
- Assets that amount to less than $35,000

Uncontested Divorce

According to the American Bar Association, an estimated 95 percent of all divorces are uncontested. This is when the two partners come to an agreement without lawyers about the property, children, and support.

LEGAL REQUIREMENTS

When you choose to get divorced, depending on your state, there are some requirements that have to be met. These requirements are:

- You must reside in your state for a specific period of time. Only a small number of states allow for non-residency divorces. Most states require that both you and your spouse, or at least one of you, have been living in the state for six months to one year. The main reason for this is so couples do not take advantage of less-stringent divorce laws in other states. For example, New York does not allow no-fault divorce. Without the residency laws for divorce, couples could go New Jersey to file for a no-fault divorce.

- You must be divorced in the state that you have been a resident of and lived in for the specified period of time required by that state, not in the state in which you were married.

- Some states require that you and your spouse have to live apart for a certain length of time before filing for divorce. The reason for this is to allow a husband and wife time to think so they can potentially reconcile before the divorce proceedings ever start.

Issues to be resolved

In every divorce, issues have to be resolved before the divorce can move forward. These issues include:

- How will debt and property be divided between the partners? There are many state and federal laws that deal with this, which can make it complicated to determine who will get what.

- Who will pay support and alimony to the other? If payments are required, how much will they be and how long before they will be paid off?

- Who will get custody of the children, and how much will child support be for the parent with custody?

THE DIVORCE PROCESS

The complete divorce process involves several steps that you should be aware of. Knowing the steps can keep you informed, and can give you a better chance of a favorable outcome.

1. The first step in divorce is separation. As mentioned, a trial separation is often required so there can be a chance of reconciliation. If you are required to have a separation period of a year, then you and your spouse must not get back together at all. If you and your wife get back together before the end of the year and stop divorce proceedings, the year will start all over again if you file for divorce in the future.

2. The next step in the process is to file a petition for divorce. This is filed in the state in which you live after you have met the separation requirements. You will complete several forms and pay a fee to file the papers at the district court in your county. If you have an attorney, he or she will complete the forms and file them for you. On the forms, you will have to fill out "grounds for divorce," which states why you are getting divorced. Even in a no-fault divorce, there has to be a reason.

3. If you are the individual filling out the divorce forms, then you need to notify your spouse with a court summons, or document. Once issued the summons, your spouse has two courses of action. She can either sign a voluntary appearance form, or she can file an answer.

a.   Voluntary appearance form: If your spouse signs this, she is agreeing to everything in the complaint and does not need to respond.

b.   File an answer: This must be filed within 20 to 30 days, after which a hearing date is set.

If your spouse is served with the divorce papers and she never responds to them, the judge will give you everything you requested in the divorce. When a summons is issued, this serves as proof to the court that you have given your spouse the notice of the divorce. The summons does the following:

a.   It tells the court clerk how to notify your spouse of the divorce.

b.   It tells the court clerk where your spouse lives.

The form of notice can also come in a variety of different forms, including:

a.   If you send it by mail, your spouse or someone acting for her needs to sign for the certified/registered mail. This serves as proof that she has received the summons. If you feel that your spouse will not pick up the mail, the sheriff can be asked to personally deliver the summons to your spouse. It costs more to do this, usually under $150, but it proves that your spouse received the summons.

b.   If you do not know where your spouse is, you can serve her by putting a summons in the local newspaper. Even if no one tells your spouse about the summons in the paper, or she does not see the summons in the paper, the court will consider that you have served her the summons.

4. Divorce trials do not happen right away, and even then can take up to a year to get started. As a result, there is often a temporary hearing held to establish certain issues, including:

    a. Custody of children and payment of child support

    b. Use of the marital home

    c. Use of the vehicles

    d. Cancelling health insurance

    e. Awarding the attorney fees of one spouse to another to pay

    f. Alimony and spousal support

5. The next step in the process is agreeing to divide the property and debts, and determining who is going to take care of the children. This is done in a written agreement without going to court. It outlines what each spouse agrees to and is legally binding as a contract. Either the spouses will do this together, or they will have attorneys involved. The reason for the agreement is to settle any issues that came up between the separation and the divorce and to get a final agreement that can be used to settle marital issues in front of a judge.

6. If the divorce goes all the way to trial, then the real battle begins. Divorce trials are held in front of a judge, without

a jury. The judge will base his or her decision on the evidence he or she receives, within a few hours at most. Some of the things the judge will decide, which are binding by law, include:

a.   Entitlement of divorce

b.   Child custody

c.   Financial and property distribution

d.   Child support

e.   Spousal support

7.   If one spouse is not happy with the decision, an appeal can be launched. If granted, the divorce goes back to the court and the entire process continues.

One aspect of divorce that is often as difficult as deciding custody is child support. For many parents, losing custody also means they need to pay child support, creating a double-whammy of emotional stress.

DEALING WITH CHILD SUPPORT

As a father, you are responsible for the welfare of your children. For the courts, that can often mean you have to provide financial support. In regards to child support, there are statistics that show the division between men and women with child support:

•   84 percent of all child support providers are men.

- Of those who pay child support, 60 percent provide money for one child, 30 percent for two children and only 10 percent support three or more children.

- Just about half of all child support providers are under the age of 40.

- The average a man pays for child support each year is $13,205.

- The average a woman pays for child support each year is $2,400.

- The average income of someone who pays child support is $42,000.

- Seventy-six percent of all people who make payments are required by court order or a child support agreement. Only 24 percent make payments without being required to do so by the courts.

- Roughly 38 percent of child support providers are responsible for other costs, including health insurance, health care costs, and medical bills.

- Only 17 percent of child support agreements have no clauses about paying for the health care of children.

- The collection of child support can be done in various different ways:

  o 33.8 percent of payments are done by withholding wages

o   31.7 percent are done by a direct payment to the parent

o   14.4 percent are done through a child support agency

o   17.7 percent are paid to the court

o   2.4 percent make up other child support payment methods

Child support is essentially the way the court makes sure that the children will be provided for in school, medicine, and other areas. Even if you and your spouse cannot talk to each other without getting angry, child support payments must be made, and the courts will see that they are paid. Child support payments must be made until the children are 18 years old, after which the payments stop.

The calculation of child support often involves complex formulas by state agencies, but it is easy enough to get a general idea. Depending on the income of the father, the amount he pays will vary, but the percentage he pays usually will not.

NUMBER OF CHILDREN	PERCENTAGE OF NET INCOME PAID IN SUPPORT
1	25
2	32
3	37
4	45

This means that if you make $38,000 in net income each year, you will pay the following:

NUMBER OF CHILDREN	AMOUNT PAID EACH YEAR
1	$9,500
2	$12,160
3	$14,060
4	$17,100

The figures above are based on if you have custody of your children 20 percent of the time. Even if you share custody in a 50/50 arrangement, you will most likely still be paying child support, but not as much as you do above.

CREATING A CHILD SUPPORT AGREEMENT

Rather than allowing the courts to decide how much is going to be paid for child support, you and your ex-partner can also work together to draw up an agreement that is fair and balanced for both of you. Often, this is better for both of you because the costs will be shared. A good way to handle child support is to have you and your ex-partner pay a certain amount based on your income. Whoever makes a higher salary pays more because he or she can afford it.

If you are paying the child support

Because you are the father, chances are you will be paying child support. That being said, there are some things you can do to ensure chid support does not become overwhelming for yourself, or something that drives you into a deep hole of debt and despair.

- First, you should pay your child support on time, every time. If you pay late, you not only get in trouble from the courts, but it can send your children the wrong message.

You may not like having to pay child support, especially if you have joint custody and your partner makes more than you do, but it is something you have to do.

- If you cannot pay all of it one month, talk to your ex-partner and give her as much as you can.

- Remember that your ex-partner may be going through a tough time financially. If she is, try to provide her with a bit more money to help out.

- Do not pay in cash. You should only pay by check because it is easier to track. Write "Child Support" along with the month and year on the memo line and keep a photocopied check in your files. Keep detailed records of the checks you write, when you sent them, and when they cleared.

- Child support cannot be deducted as payment on taxes, so it is best not to try.

If you are receiving child support

Although mothers receive child support more often than not, there is a chance that you will receive child support. If you do receive child support, there are a few things that you should remember.

- The children should never be used as a way to collect money. Children need their mothers, and using lack of child support as a tool to turn them against her is wrong.

- Child support is there to help you, so do not feel guilty about taking it. You need it for the kids, and only the kids are going to be using it, so there is no reason to feel guilty.

- Keep records of when you receive payment and how much each payment was.

- Keep an accurate log of how all the payments are spent.

- Child support is not declared on taxes.

If you find that you are not being paid child support, there are avenues you can pursue:

- Go to the county district attorney. By law, the district attorney is required to help parents with custody for free. You can also talk to your attorney.

- Visit the Web site of the Federal Office of Child Support Enforcement through the U.S. Department of Health and Human Services Administration for Children and Families at **www.acf.hhs.gov/programs/cse**, or call the office at 202-401-9373.

CHAPTER CONCLUSION

Dealing with custody, child support, and other legal issues is a serious issue for many fathers. When a relationship falls apart, even if it is the fault of the father, it can be an earth-shattering event. What was once loved is now lost, and the father's entire life is about to change.

Custody and child support, unfortunately, tend to go against the father. A minority of 'deadbeat' fathers have caused the majority to face the stigma. The truth is that there are many fathers, the vast majority, who are devoted to their children and want to help provide them with everything they need in life. While you may not get the custody you want, the important thing is to enjoy the time you have with your children and leave as big an impact on their lives as you can.

Child support can be a tough financial anchor around your neck, but it is necessary to ensure that your children are cared for. If your partner makes more money than you, your attorney should be able to negotiate a cheaper rate for you, making it easier to pay.

In Chapter 2, the kids will be addressed. Usually, the children are the ones who are impacted the most when parents divorce. It is important to make them feel at ease and to help them understand that it is not their fault.

2

Helping the Kids Cope

> *"When it is time to part, then it is time to part. There should be no regrets. The beauty of marriage is like the fleeting perfection of a snowflake."*
>
> — Deng Ming-Dao, Chinese author and philosopher

When children go through the divorce of their parents, it can be a traumatic event in their lives. Up to that moment, they may have thought everything was fine and that their parents would never part. The cold reality of divorce can leave a lasting impression on children and change them in many ways far into the future. For them, few things other than a death of a parent or sibling are as devastating as the divorce of their parents. This is why it is incredibly important for you, as the father, to ensure they get through it easily. The divorce is not their fault, and they should not be drawn into it.

TELLING THE CHILDREN ABOUT THE DIVORCE

One of the hardest parts of divorce is not always coming to the decision to divorce — often, that can be an easy decision depending on the circumstances. The hardest part is telling the children about the divorce. Roughly 80 percent of all children younger than 5 years old from divorced parents had no idea that a divorce was about to take place. It was completely unexpected.

It is imperative to make one point clear: Unless you are certain that you are separating or getting divorced, do not get the kids involved. For a young child, or children, it is emotionally devastating to have parents come to them every few months saying there is going to be a divorce. Eventually, as the children grow older, they will stop believing there will be a divorce.

When you are about to break the news to the kids, follow these tips to make it easier on them:

1. Agree with your partner prior to the discussion that there will be absolutely no arguing.

2. Do not schedule anything else for that day, as it may take some time to tell the children and answer all the questions they may have.

3. Ensure that the children are fully awake and thinking clearly. The evening is not a good time, but Saturday afternoon is.

4. Be ready with a list of all the things you want to tell the children about the divorce. It can be fine to talk about divorce with your ex-partner, but it is a completely different

circumstance when you are staring at your children, trying to tell them why there is going to be a divorce.

5. Do not tell your children about the divorce by yourself. You should have your ex-partner there with you. This will help so a "bad guy" is not identified, no one will receive blame, it will show you and your ex-partner cooperating, the children will be more comfortable, and the children will not feel pressured to take sides.

6. Tell the children at the home, nowhere else. Taking them to the zoo to help make it easier could cause your children to start hating the zoo because of the memory associated with it.

Once you have all this in place, you can begin to tell them. To make it easier for them, follow the following course of action. It will help make the entire process better for you, as well.

1. Get right to the point and tell the children that you and their mother are not going to be living together anymore. If they are old enough to know what a divorce is, you can tell them that you are getting divorced.

2. Do not sugarcoat anything. Tell them that their lives are going to change and cover the things that will change the most, including who they may be living with and how often they will see each parent.

3. Tell them that both you and their mother will always be emotionally supportive, and if they need to talk about the divorce, all they have to do is ask. Tell them you and their mother will love them always, no matter what.

4. Do not make promises you cannot keep, or lie to them. This will only make the entire process more difficult for your children.

5. Tell them outright that it is not their fault and that you are sorry. It is very important that you apologize because the children typically feel that they are the ones to blame for the divorce.

6. Be ready to answer their questions such as, "Will you still love me?" or, "Why do not you love Mommy anymore?"

7. Explain to them the truth of why the divorce is happening, even if it was your fault, but you do not want to admit it.

THE FIRST FEW DAYS

Over the course of the next few days, your children will begin to start dealing and coping with the news of the divorce. There is no one pattern that all children will follow when dealing with divorce. Each child will deal with the news of the divorce differently. However, you can help them through these next few difficult days by doing the following:

1. Let your children react in any way that works for them. Expecting them to react to the news in a certain way will only put pressure on them.

2. Always be ready to talk with your children and let them know, over and over, that you are there to talk if they want to.

3.   Keep routines the same. Introducing too much change all at once can be overwhelming for the children.

4.   Do not be afraid of letting your children see you cry. If they see you cry, they will see it is all right to express their emotions and they may be more willing to talk to you.

TALKING ABOUT THE DIVORCE AROUND THE KIDS

There is a common belief that once the divorce is mentioned to the kids, that is all that needs to be done. Parents think kids are too fragile to handle the thought of the divorce and there should be no talk about it; however, this is the wrong course of action. While you and your ex-spouse should never fight in front of the children, argue about the divorce, or draw the children into it, there is nothing wrong with talking about the divorce with them around. This not only helps the children understand the divorce, but it can also put them at ease to see their mother and father talking about the divorce in a calm and civil manner.

If a mother and father suddenly stop talking when the children walk into the room, the children are going to realize that something is wrong. A child's imagination is a powerful tool and they may think Mom and Dad are fighting. This presents the problem of assumptions. The parents may not have been angry at all, only talking in a civil manner about how to go about the separation, but their child may see it differently because of the assumption of their parents fighting. This creates unneeded stress for the child.

Hiding things from your children to protect them has the opposite effect. They may start to believe that the divorce may not be happening; giving them false hope that everything will return to normal.

It may also, as was outlined in the example above, give them the belief that their parents are fighting when they are not. Children, for better or worse, are part of the divorce process. While they should not be tools or pawns in a divorce, they should know what is going on. The children need to be off to the side in the divorce, but they do not need to have their eyes and ears covered. Parents want to protect their children, but trying to protect them from the divorce is the wrong strategy.

ELIMINATING THEIR GUILT

When a child is first told that his or her parents are divorcing, the child will go through many emotions. The most common are confusion, fear, sadness, anger, shock, and, of course, guilt. Guilt is very common for children who have gone through a parental divorce. One of the main reasons is that children do not fully grasp or understand how their parents could no longer love each other and choose to divorce. When this happens, children lose the ability to trust themselves, and they begin to question why the divorce happened. This naturally leads them to the conclusion that they are responsible for the divorce. The thought process for a child dealing with the news usually looks something like this:

"My parents love each other"

"If my parents are getting divorced, but love each other, then there is another reason"

"I am the reason my parents are getting divorced"

This is a generalization of how a child will feel with divorce, but it is essentially how it works in their minds. They cannot understand why their parents do not love each other anymore, and they cannot understand why they are not living together. If someone is leaving, or if the child is being passed between parents due to custody, it is only natural for the child to feel that the divorce is somehow his or her fault. This is where the guilt comes in. Because children often feel guilty about the divorce, even though they have nothing to do with the divorce, it is important to show they are not at fault.

Show them it is not their fault

It is very important that both you and your ex-partner work together to show the children that the divorce is not their fault. Spend time with the children, make them happy, smile, and even spend time together as a family, showing them that the issues that created the divorce have nothing to do with them. Even if you and your ex-partner hate each other at that point, put on a smile and make your children feel good. Do not hide the divorce from them, but do not involve them in it either. Do not talk about all the things that your ex-partner did wrong. Also, do not talk with your children or ex-partner about how great things were when you were first dating or first married. Your children may hear this and begin to feel that if things were great when their parents were first married and are not great now, the only thing that changed was their birth. This will take them down the road to guilt again. Although it is important to make them happy, do not spoil them. Spoiling your children can send the wrong message and may show them that you are feeling guilty about the divorce.

Mom and Dad still love them

Showing your children that divorce is not their fault is important, but it is also important to show your children that both you and their mother love them. If they feel loved, your children will be more likely to cope better with the divorce and not feel guilty about it. Do not spoil your children with presents in an effort to over compensate. Instead, hug them, tell them you love them, and tell them you will always be there to talk to them about any questions they may have. If you hide from them because of your own guilt, your children may think that you are hiding from them because they are guilty.

Signs of guilt

There are certain signs of guilt in children that it is important to watch for and to deal with before the feelings of guilt manifest into something worse, like self-destructive behavior.

- Your child may regress to an early age or mentality. This means that your child may start acting like he or she is two years old, even if he or she is five. One of the reasons for this is that children want to revert to the way things were when they were younger, before the divorce. Out of guilt, they begin to act younger to recreate those happier times.

- Children who feel guilty will often make deals with their parents on the promise of being good. They think that the divorce is happening because of them, so in their mind, everything will be fine if they are good.

- Your child may begin to feel that he or she is somehow flawed or defective and will develop a poor self-esteem, which will be evident in how the child acts toward himself or herself.

- Sleep problems may develop in your child, and he or she may wake up several times in a night to ensure that the parents have not abandoned him or her.

- Anxiety can begin to develop; by extension, aggression and temper tantrums can come about, too.

- Your child may seem more irritable than usual. He or she is not angry with you, but angry with himself or herself over guilt.

Often, the signs of guilt can be confused with signs of stress in children. While it can be hard to determine if your child feels guilty or is just worried, it is important to always support him or her and show that you love him or her through it all.

SIGNS OF DIVORCE STRESS IN KIDS

Stress is an awful thing to have. It can lead to serious problems with health, and it can even hurt the mental well-being of an individual. Stress commonly causes individuals to break down. In short, stress is terrible at any age and for any person. This is why it is so important to watch for stress signs in your children. These signs are as follows:

Toddlers

- The child will not want to eat or nurse. This will be most evident as the child chooses not to eat the foods that he or she previously liked.

- The child will cry more than is common for a child his or her age. You should know how much your child usually cries, and you will know when he or she cries more than usual.

- The child will be irritated by small things. These will be things that did not irritate him or her before.

- The child will have a changing sleep pattern. He or she will either not fall asleep until late, or start sleeping well into the morning. He or she may also start waking up more during the night and be more irritated about going to sleep.

Ages 3 to 5

- The child will not eat as much as he or she normally does.

- The child will get very angry when things do not go his or her way.

- There will be increased instances of the child being sick with headaches, stomach pains, or a cold.

- The child will not want to go to bed at night, or will have more nightmares and trouble sleeping throughout the night.

- The child may cling more to you or your ex-partner.

- The child may start to have more accidents. These can include bed wetting or not wanting to go to the toilet, resulting in wetting his or her pants — this is due to regression. Also in regards to regression, the child will start to use baby talk.

- The child will not do as he or she is told and may begin to talk back.

- The child will pout more than before, and the pouting will last for longer periods of time.

Age 6 to 12

- The child may develop problems with his or her friends and may have more confrontations with teachers. Teachers will let you know about changed behavior, and you will notice friends are not hanging around as much.

- The child will stop participating in extracurricular activities.

- The child's school work will begin to suffer. A child who once had grades in the A's and B's will typically become a C student.

- The child will not be able to sleep at night.

- The child will develop more colds, headaches, and other types of infections due to the stress on his or her body. This also results in a weakened immune system.

- The child will start wetting the bed again.

Teenagers

- The teenager's grades will begin to suffer. Grades will often drop during a divorce, but when he or she really takes a plunge, stress is to blame.

- The teenager will start to act out more on a regular basis, often becoming aggressive to you or your ex-partner.

- The teenager may develop a problem with drugs, which is used as an escape from the stress and anxiety of the divorce going on around him or her.

- The teenager may drop his or her old friends in favor of hanging out with a bad crowd. He or she finds acceptance in the crowd, which may be something lacking at home due to the divorce.

Ways to manage

There are ways you can manage the stress in your child's life and keep it from becoming a serious problem for him or her. While you may not get rid of all the stress, helping your child with it can make a big change.

For children just born to the age of 12, there are several things you can do:

- Spend as much quality time with your children as you possibly can. Anything from reading them a story, cuddling with them, going out for a day together, or just giving them a hug will make a big impact on the lives of your children during the divorce.

- Take more time with them at bedtime so they have an easier time falling asleep.

- Talk to them about stress — how it can affect them and where it comes from. The more they understand it, the better able they will be to manage it.

- Watch for the signs of stress in your children. When you see them, talk to them about it and show that you understand why they are stressed.

For children ages 12 onward, you can do the following to help your teenagers manage their stress.

- Participate in school events and activities with your teenager. Your teenager may not always like you hanging around, but it can help him or her feel more of a bond with you that can decrease stress.

- Always be ready to talk to your teenager whenever he or she wants to talk to you. Never put up a closed door and always be ready to sit down with him or her to work through whatever the teenager is going through.

- Ask your teenager about his or her life and friends. Do not be nosy, but the more you understand about him or her, the more able you are to help.

- Talk to your teenager about your own struggles and stories from your youth. That way, he or she will feel more comfortable with you because he or she will know you went through similar things.

- Never use judgmental tones of voice or put down your teenager, even if you are arguing. This will only add to the feelings of stress.

- Keep an even temper with your teenager and always use a positive approach to the problem of what he or she is dealing with.

CASE STUDY: THERAPY FOR KIDS

Carole Lieberman, M.D
Expert witness * Psychiatrist
On the clinical faculty at University
of California Los Angeles

I am a psychiatrist and expert witness. I provide psychotherapy for children of divorce, as well as for children and adults with other problems. I also do custody evaluations and give testimony in divorce and custody cases, as well as other civil and criminal matters. Fees for a psychiatric expert witness in divorce and/or custody cases can range from $15,000 (if parents agree on issues) to $100,000 or more (if there are ongoing disputes and more than one child).

Children of divorce need psychotherapy, at least for six to 12 months after the divorce, if not longer. Otherwise, the psychological scars of divorce can last a lifetime. Parents should agree on a custody arrangement as soon as possible — one that has the best interests of the children in mind. Both parents should put their children's needs before their own to make the divorce less traumatic.

Even in the best circumstances where the divorce is less contentious, the impact on children is still devastating. It leaves scars for life unless children are put immediately into psychotherapy as soon as parents are contemplating divorce. Divorce has the worst impact when a parent abandons the children emotionally, even if not physically. This most often happens when one or both parents have a lover. It is especially devastating for little girls when Daddy has a girlfriend, and especially difficult for little boys when Mommy has a boyfriend, though it is difficult even for children of the same gender. When one parent has a new lover, they consciously or inadvertently focus too much attention on the lover, and the child feels rejected and abandoned.

The emotional scars left on children of divorce can include: depression, anxiety, learning problems, nightmares, separation anxiety, problems forming relationships with the opposite sex when they grow up, and more. The trauma of separation and divorce causes children to grow up being fearful of close attachments. They fear that if they befriend or love someone, it will only end in the same disappointment, anger, and abandonment that their parents' marriage did. These scars can be ameliorated, if not totally prevented, by intensive psychotherapy.

Of course, other issues that cause or are related to divorce impact the children as well, such as financial deprivation, substance abuse, depression, anxiety, domestic violence, and so on.

A divorced father needs to find a good family law attorney and an experienced psychiatric expert witness, both with winning records. A father needs to show that he is truly interested in being there for his children, not just in punishing his ex or lowering his child support payments. He needs to make every effort to speak to his children every day; give them cute cards and meaningful gifts; show interest and attend their games, plays, and other school activities; take them to the doctor; know their favorite foods and anything else that is important to them; and see them every moment that their ex allows until custody arrangements are ordered by the court.

If the divorce is instigated by the father, the divorce has less of an impact on the father than if the wife instigates the divorce, because he feels less emasculated. If the father is truly devoted to his children, he will be devastated either way. But if he is thinking more of himself than his children, he will soon forget about their needs.

There is no one-size-fits-all best custody arrangement. Each situation is unique, since each father, mother, and child are unique — with their own individual personalities, needs, and problems. Each child needs to spend at least some time with each parent. However, if sexual, physical, or emotional abuse, neglect, domestic violence, mental illness, addiction, or some other serious problem exists, the visitation should be supervised and treatment should be ordered for the parent and child.

CHAPTER CONCLUSION

The hardest part of divorce for a father is breaking the news to his children and explaining the divorce process to them. No father wants to do this because fathers love their children and only want them to be happy. In a divorce, however, it is hard to make sure your children are happy. This is why it is so important to talk with your children and help them realize that what is happening is not their fault. They are not to blame and they should not feel guilty about what is going on. Too often during a divorce, parents will focus on each other and trying to ensure they do not lose out in the divorce process. Often, the children are on the sidelines watching with no support or help. It is incredibly important that you and your ex-partner work together to help your children feel more at ease and to show them that no matter what happens and no matter where they live, they will be loved by both of you forever.

CHAPTER 3

Working With Your Ex-Spouse

> *"We lov'd, and we lov'd as long as we could*
> *'Till our love was lov'd out in us both;*
> *But our marriage is dead, when the pleasure is fled:*
> *'Twas pleasure first made it an oath."*
>
> — John Dryden, Marriage à la Mode, English poet

Often in a divorce, the thought of working with an ex-partner is a foreign concept. Either both parties are too hurt or angry to think about it, or it is not the best method to ensure an amicable divorce, or it is not the best method to ensure a proper environment for the children.

Working with your ex-partner is beneficial for many reasons. It can ensure a smoother divorce and a chance of friendship after the divorce. The kids will cope with the divorce easier and there will be rules and boundaries set by the two of you, ensuring the children are being raised in the same manner at both households.

DO NOT BLAME YOUR EX-PARTNER

In the last chapter, the issue of blaming your ex-partner for the divorce in front of the children was addressed. However, it is also important that the blame game does not go on between you even when the children are not present. When you are both blaming each other, you will not make progress, feelings will be hurt, and resentment will only grow.

There are several reasons you may blame your ex-partner:

- Your ex-partner may not be around to defend herself, making it easy to blame her.

- You may have caused the divorce and, instead of blaming yourself, you are shifting the blame to your ex-partner.

- You are angry because your partner caused the divorce and you want to blame her for it.

When you blame your ex-partner, either in her presence or by yourself, you are not helping matters. Even if you know your ex-partner blames you, it is best just to take the high road. Not blaming your ex-partner can go a long way. First, if your ex-partner knows that you do not blame her, it may make it easier for her to forgive herself, or forgive you. Once that happens, the goal of having a happy friendship after the divorce becomes much easier to achieve. On the flip side, if your partner wants to work with you and all you can do is blame her, it will not help matters move forward. Blame holds everything back during and after a relationship. It is impossible to have any sort of arrangement or friendship after a divorce if blame is still around. The sooner you and your ex-partner move beyond blame, the better off everyone will be.

ELIMINATING THE BLAME GAME

At first, it may seem like a good idea to blame your partner in front of the children, especially if you see the divorce as a battle you want to win, with custody as the ultimate prize. If your children say they want to live with you in front of the judge, it can go a long way to get you custody. However, what are you sacrificing to do this? It is completely possible for couples to not only have an amicable divorce, but to be friends afterward. For the children, this is the most beneficial outcome from the divorce.

It is not your partner's fault

While you may feel it is your partner's fault and you may blame her for everything that went wrong in the relationship, you should not tell the children. This is an opinion that you will have in your own head, and that is where it stays when you are around the children. It does not matter if your partner committed adultery, or if she handed you the divorce papers and you feel like the victim; you must present a united front in front of your children. The children have to know that while their mom and dad are not together, they will not be used as pawns in the fight over the divorce. It can be especially hard not to blame your partner when you have no one to talk to but the kids. That being said, the kids do not need to hear it and you do not need to tell them. The children will manage through the divorce much easier if there is no blaming between their mother and father.

Talking with your partner

While you can ensure that you will not blame your partner, you cannot guarantee that your partner will do the same. This is why it is important to talk with your partner about the situation over the divorce and the children. Explain that while neither of you are happy about the divorce, the children take priority.

Your partner may agree with you, or she may not. All you can do is talk with her and show her the importance of making the children feel at ease and keeping them out of the divorce fight. Hopefully, by talking about it with your partner, you can keep the blame game from happening on the other end, as well.

CREATING BOUNDARIES

When raising children, boundaries and rules are vital. In a divorce where children are involved, boundaries are just as important, if not more so. When the children are being raised in two different households, there can be two different systems in place, which can lead to a great deal of confusion for the children. When one parent does not respect the rules put in place by another parent, it creates a hostile environment where one parent feels the other is undermining his or her authority. To have a friendly relationship with your ex-partner, understanding and respecting each others' boundaries can make for a friendly relationship after the divorce. A friendly relationship makes for happier children and a less stressful atmosphere for all.

Rules on visits

Visitations can be a stressful affair for a father. When he is going to pick up his children, he may have to deal with an ex-partner he is not happy seeing. To make visitations easier for both you and your ex-partner, having rules in place can make the entire process easier. Some rules that ex-partners should work out include:

1. Avoid talking about the ex-partner in front of the chil-
    dren or attempting to get information about her life from
    the children.

2. Keep the same rules in place for the children no matter
    where they are staying for the night.

3. Do not try to turn the children against the other parent
    through spoiling them or putting down the other parent.

To ensure that your ex-partner does not feel like you do not take
visitations seriously, or that you are using them in a way she dis-
agrees with, follow these tips for what you should do:

*   Always show up on time. Your children are accustomed
    to the routine, and a lot of planning has gone into the fact
    that you are taking the children that weekend. It sends the
    wrong message to your children if you do not show up on
    time and your ex-partner can use that against you.

*   Assure your partner that you do have a plan for the child
    that involves more than just watching television.

*   Do not rush away when you pick up your children. Make
    it easier for them in the transition by taking your time
    and even talking to your ex-partner before leaving. Even
    though you are divorced, the kids will like seeing their
    parents talking to each other.

*   Assure your ex-partner that you will be a good role model
    and that there will be no drinking, swearing, or rude
    behavior in front of the children.

No contradicting

One of the biggest areas parents fail in is through contradiction. While it can be normal to feel like you must put down your ex-partner to get the children to your side, it is the wrong course of action. In no way should you contradict your ex-partner. Sometimes it can be innocent enough. For example, you may decide to take the children to get some ice cream at night. When they tell you that Mom does not allow sweets after 6 p.m., it can be innocent enough to say, "Oh, I think this time we can." You do not mean to contradict your ex-partner, you are just trying to show the kids a fun time. The problem with this is the contradiction between parents, and you run into the problem of being the "Disneyland Dad." A Disneyland Dad is the dad who does all the fun things with the kids, leaving the mother to be the bad guy by putting rules in place. The kids will, of course, love visiting their father in this case because it is like a mini-vacation from rules, but it will destroy any chance of a friendly relationship between the mother and father.

If the children are not allowed to have ice cream past 6 p.m. with their mother, then there is no ice cream past 6 p.m. with you. These are the rules that need to be explained and listed so both of you have an understanding of what is allowed and what is not allowed.

Some of the things that should be discussed between the two of you include:

- Bedtimes
- What they can or should eat
- Having friends over
- Homework
- Video games/Internet time/television time

- Talking about the other parent
- The activities that are planned
- Extracurricular activities
- Health issues
- Allowance

FINDING THINGS TO AGREE ON

A common method of mediation involves not having disagreeing parties agree on something, but instead finding ways for the parties to see the similarities between them. This method of mediation is very effective and useful when ex-spouses are trying to find a way to talk to each other in an effort to help the children. By solving the minor problems that may come up, it can be easier to solve the major problems that cause the real stress. Cooperation is essential when raising kids in two different homes.

Too often, individuals will focus on what does not work, rather than what does work. In a relationship, focusing on what does not work leads to the end of the relationship. This is how the divorce can happen. After the divorce, the relationship is gone, and what did not make it work is also gone. Now it is time to focus on what did make it work. There was a time when you and your partner worked together, loved each other, and wanted to be together forever. There had to be a foundation for that, and that is the foundation where you can start building a new friendship, rather than marriage. By finding things to agree on, you can compromise.

Some of the things you and your ex-partner can agree on are:

- Both of you only want the best for the children

- Both of you want the children to do well in school

- Both of you love the children and want them to be happy

- Both of you want the children to live in a stress-free environment

- Both of you want the children to have good role models

- Both of you want the children to learn about rules, limits, and the difference between right and wrong

Now that there is a list of the things both of you agree on, there can be cooperation on other issues. With this list, it is possible to find cooperation in the following manner:

- Both of you only want the best for the children

  - The two of you will pool money together for the children to ensure they have the best of everything.

- Both of you want the children to do well in school

  - The two of you will support the children in school and other activities by helping with homework, going to their events, and supporting them equally.

- Both of you love the children and want them to be happy

  - The two of you will show your love by respecting the children and their other parent. You will also not draw the children into any arguments about the divorce or use them as pawns.

- Both of you want the children in a stress-free environment

- The two of you will not fight or argue in front of the children.

• Both of you want the children to have good role models

- The two of you will act respectful and kind to each other to show the children how they should act with others, and how to take the high road.

• Both of you want the children to learn about rules, limits, and the difference between right and wrong.

- The two of you will have a list of rules and boundaries set up that the children will follow, no matter what home they are in.

LEARN TO COMPROMISE

Many parents see divorce as a battle that never ends. From the first day the divorce papers are presented, there is a constant battle between mothers and fathers to win. While many divorces do go well, many are like a war with children caught in the cross-fire. In this kind of environment, it can be hard to think about compromising. Many parents feel that if they compromise, they are somehow giving in. Once again, this is the wrong way to think about things. Compromise is good for both the mother and father, and it is especially good for the children.

When you compromise on the small things, you are giving yourself bargaining power on the bigger things. The following is an example to illustrate the importance of compromise:

Your ex-spouse is going out with friends at 6 p.m. on Friday, but you usually do not pick up the children until 8 p.m. on Fridays. While it may feel nice to tell her that you are not going to pick up the kids until 8 p.m. and she will just have to rework her social life, this is neither thinking ahead nor thinking clearly. This is anger and hurt talking. Your logical mind is not working in this case. Instead of saying "no," you should say "Yes, that is not a problem. Have fun tonight. If you want, I can pick the kids up at 5:30 p.m. so you have an easier time getting ready."

Did you give in? Did you admit defeat? No, you gave your ex-spouse what she wanted and a bit more. That little extra effort gave you some extra good points with your ex-partner, and that can go a long way. Now when you need something, she may be more willing to help out. If you show willingness to compromise and help out, your ex-partner may be willing to negotiate better custody arrangements with the children. Winning the small battles is not important. Divorce is not war, although it can feel like it. What is important is helping out your ex-partner for the kids.

Sharing the financial burden

When a mother needs some extra money and the father helps, it can forge a strong friendship after the divorce. Sometimes child support may not be enough at certain times of the year. If a father makes $67,000 a year, and pays more than $21,000 in child support for the two children, it amounts to $1,750 a month. If the mother works as a waitress and only makes $1,000 a month, then she may have to stretch the budget during birthdays, holidays, and the start of the school year. In this case, there is nothing wrong with paying a bit extra if you can afford it.

The cost of raising two children is a little more than $20,000 a year. Sometimes extra costs come up, and if the mother cannot pay for that, then as the child's father you need to help out if you can. As the children get older, the cost to raise them goes up, but child support does not always change. Inflation can also come into play, which is not always taken into account with child support.

Share the financial burden with your ex-partner by doing the following:

1. Pay for half of the school supplies. As time goes on, school supplies will cost more, and a mother on a fixed income may not be able to afford them all.

2. During the December holiday season, help buy some extra presents from the children. Not just presents from yourself, but presents from both you and your ex-partner.

3. If the children are involved in sports, it can cost extra money to enroll them and pay for their equipment. Hockey and football need a lot of equipment, which can cost hundreds of dollars. Do not deny your kids sports just because you do not want to share the burden.

4. During Halloween and Easter, help buy the kids some extra treats with your ex-partner to make those holidays a bit more special.

5. Share the cost of putting on a big birthday for the children. Help pay for the cost of the party, as well as the presents.

When you share the financial burden, you are not just helping your ex-partner, you are also helping your children.

Going to the kids' events

Children these days have plenty of extra-curricular activities. From sports to plays, from swimming to recitals, kids are extremely busy. For children, something like a baseball game or a recital is very important to them. They want their family to see them, which means having their mother and father watching them, even if their parents are divorced.

Showing support for the children after a divorce is important for the well-being of the child. The child will be proud that both his or her parents are out to see him or her, and even if you do not sit together, it is sending the right message. You are showing your ex-partner that you do care for the children enough to be there with her, and you are showing the child that no matter what happens with his or her parents, they will always love the child and support him or her.

Being civil with each other

There may be times that you want to scream at your partner, call her names, or just be angry, but this is bad for you and your children. Grudges are things that you should not carry with you for your entire life. Eventually, it comes time for you to let things go and accept that things have changed. When an individual can get past a grudge, it is possible to move forward unhindered.

When two ex-spouses act civilly to each other, whether in front of the children or not, it is beneficial to all involved. If a father goes on the war path with his ex-wife and screams at her, her feelings of anger and anxiety will severely affect her relationship with him and the children's relationship with him. Acting civil helps you feel better and will help your relationship with your ex-partner. You feel happier because you can be nicer, and your ex-partner will feel better knowing that the bad feelings of the divorce may now be passing.

The two of you loved each other once, and possibly a part of each of you still loves the other person, which is often why there is anger and resentment. It is important to draw upon that piece of love and use it to create a civil friendship after the divorce. Children who have divorced parents who act friendly to each other will feel better about their parents and will be well-adjusted as a result.

CHAPTER CONCLUSION

Many fathers are surprised when they are told that to be a good father, working with the ex-wife is important. They feel that they have been hurt, wronged, or scrutinized by the court system and her lawyers — why should they choose to be civil or to help their ex-partner? As with anything in the life of a father, it is all for the children's benefit. If a child sees his or her parents acting civil with each other, working together, and helping each other, the child will feel happier and less stressed.

The divorce is over, you have gone your separate ways, and the only thing linking the two of you now is the children. Why damage that one link with petty grievances and grudges? Rise above and work together for that link, for your children. Help each other with finances relating to the children, go to children's events, and work with each other. Show your children that while you do not live together anymore, you will always work together for them.

4 | Widowhood

> *"Widow. The word consumes itself."*
>
> — Sylvia Plath, American writer

Throughout this section, divorce has been dissected. Statistically, fathers usually become single fathers due to divorce, rather than the death of a wife. Widowers, or men whose wives have died, are rare. According to the U.S. Census Bureau, of the 2.5 million single fathers in the United States, 42 percent are divorced, 38 percent were never married, 16 percent are separated, and only 4 percent are widowed. This means that of 2.5 million single fathers, 100,000 are widowers.

Many American men have become single fathers not because of the breakdown of their marriages, but the unexpected loss of their partners. Therefore, it is important that the topic of widowhood is also covered.

THE FIVE STAGES OF GRIEF

Nearly everyone knows the five stages of grief. Created by Elisabeth Kübler-Ross in her book *On Death and Dying* in 1969, the Kübler-Ross Model of grief has become the template for how people tend to grieve for a loved one, as well as if they have been diagnosed with a terminal disease. The five stages are denial, anger, bargaining, depression, and acceptance.

Denial

This is the stage the brain creates as a way of forming a defense for you and your mental well-being. Common thoughts during this stage include:

- "I feel fine."
- "This is not happening."
- "I am okay, everything is all right."

Eventually, this stage passes because there is no escaping the fact that you are not fine and this is indeed happening. The death happened, and you have to face it to be able to move on with your grief. During this stage, there will also be a heightened awareness of situations and the individuals who will be left behind after one dies.

Anger

In this stage, you recognize that there is no way you can keep denying that the death happened. As a result, you will become angry and have feelings of both rage and envy. Those individuals who come to symbolize life and happiness will cause resentment and jealousy in you. Common things that are said in this stage include:

- "Why did this happen to me? This is not fair!"

- "How could this happen?"

- "Who should I blame for this?"

- "This is not my fault!"

Bargaining

Once you pass from anger, you will move to bargaining. This is more common if you are facing a terminal illness, but it can happen with the death of a spouse. You will want to bargain for the death not to be true, that it is not actually happening. Often, this stage involves negotiating with a higher power. Some things that are often said in this stage include:

- "Let it not be true; I will do anything."
- "Please let her be alive."

Depression

This is a dangerous stage because it can result in you not moving out of it and staying depressed for a long period of time. Many times, an individual will stay in the depression stage for quite a while, but it is important to naturally move out of it through whatever helps them. If you want to talk, then talk to people about your grief. If you prefer to be reserved, grieve on your own. If you want to talk to a group, join a group support program. This is critical for the next stage, which is the most important of all the stages (acceptance). Some things often said in this stage include:

- "Nothing will ever be the same again, so why bother with anything?"

- "All that I loved is gone. I do not want to live anymore."

- "I want things to be the way they were before and that is not possible, so I cannot move on."

Acceptance

- This is the stage where you reach your peace and understanding with the death of your spouse. At this point, you will probably want to be left alone, but you will be feeling better and the grief will more or less have passed. At this point, you are no longer struggling with the grief, and you have accepted it. Once you reach this point, you are past the hardest part and are ready to move on with your life. Some things often said in this stage include:

- "It is going to be okay."

- "I can move on now."

- "I accept what happened, and now I can live anew."

CASE STUDY: DEALING
WITH GRIEF

Suzy Yehl Marta, Grief & loss expert
Author of Healing the Hurt, Restoring
the Hope
Founder of Rainbows for All Children

I believe that it is more difficult for men to get over divorce or death because, culturally, they have been brought up to feel that they should fix problems or have the right answers. What divorce and death teach us is that, as humans, there are some things in life that we cannot fix, change, or repair.

Additionally, society has conditioned men to keep that stiff upper lip, to hold in their emotions, and to be strong for everyone around them. Furthermore, most men do not have a circle of friends that they can be vulnerable with about anything. So, during those times of loss, the dad does not have a confidant to walk beside him as he grieves his loss or a significant change.

In my book, *Healing The Hurt, Restoring The Hope*, there is help, wisdom, and ideas to help a single dad understand his children's grief and also to be a positive support to them so they can heal well. Some of my musts for helping children grieve include:

• Stay active and present in your child's life. Never, ever give up or walk away from your child, no matter how difficult it is for you. Keep in mind the father must be mature and always take the high road for his kids' sake.

• Buy your kids books about the type of loss the family is experiencing. Read them to yourself first, and then read them to the younger ones. If the children are older than eight, give them the book to read. Once the book as been read by the kids, talk about them as a family or individually. Ask the child if he or she has ever felt like the characters in the book. This is a gentle, non-threatening way to open up a conversation between father and child.

• Hold "family time," when the dad has set aside quality time once a week to check in on the kids' emotions. It allows the father to get a pulse on his kids' well-being, and it lets the kids know he cares and they can turn to him when the hurt is interfering with life. The journey of grief takes years for everyone, but the dad needs to know that his children will reopen and revisit the loss or change at all of life's benchmarks.

• Be candid with the kids about how Dad is hurting too. This gives them permission to acknowledge and feel their own emotions. The dad can do this without being dependent on his children or saying negative things about his former spouse.

• Seek a grief support group for children in the community where they live. These groups are not counseling or therapy, but rather an emotional refuge for the children to feel ordinary because they will be surrounded by peers their own age experiencing the same type of loss.

It is critical that the children talk about their loss or change with others their own age in a setting where they are guided by an adult who has taken some type of training on grief and loss.

Grief is a normal reaction to a significant loss or change in one's life. The intensity and length of the grief periods are dependent on how much someone has invested in or loved what is now gone. Grief is a constellation of emotions that is often conflicting. It is physical, emotional, and spiritual, and it affects everyone differently.

Grieving takes a long time — three to five years — and that is if one is really working through his grief and does his work. If someone denies that the feelings exist or pushes them aside, it certainly can prolong the grief experience. Often, men seek another relationship too quickly, which only delays the inevitable of doing the grief work. For each of us, it takes as long as it takes. The important fact is that one keeps moving through myriad emotions of grief and does not stay stuck in one phase.

GRIEVING ALONE

It is extremely difficult to go through the loss of a loved one, especially your partner, when there are children involved. In this regard, it can feel good to grieve alone, to hide your grief, and to reserve it for times when you can cry on your own or grieve in your own way. It is important to remember that everyone grieves differently. Some cry, and others bottle it up. Some continue on as they always have because there is comfort in routine, while others choose to seek friends and family for support. There is no right way to grieve. The important thing is that you grieve because grief helps you to move on and to put the tragedy behind you. It will never leave your mind, but it will fade into the background and the pain will diminish.

HOW KIDS GRIEVE

Your kids are going to grieve, and they may grieve very hard for a long time. As their father, you need to be there to grieve with them. They need to be shown that you understand their grief and that you grieve yourself. The worst thing you can do is to shut yourself off from everything to grieve.

There are some important points to remember when kids must grieve the loss of a mother:

1. If kids are old enough, usually around five to six years old, they will understand the concept of death. They see it every night on the news, television shows, movies, and games. Death is not a stranger to them. They understand what it is, but they have probably never experienced it personally. The children may have had a pet that died, or even lost a grandparent, but losing a mother is especially hard; they will initially feel several emotions.

   a. **Anger:** They may be angry because their mother left them. This can happen when the mother has committed suicide, or when the mother has died as the result of an illness or accident.

   b. **Sadness:** They will have an overwhelming feeling of sadness and will feel sorry for themselves as a way of coping.

   c. **Confusion:** They will be confused about their emotions and may begin to get irritable and lash out at the only person who can understand what they are going through at that moment: you.

2.   Kids will not grieve in a typical manner. This is something they have never gone through to that degree, and that will cause them to act very odd. Some of the behavior changes that may occur in your children following the death of their mother include:

a. **Bed-wetting:** In an effort to make things like they were in the past, the child will regress, no different than they do in a divorce.

b. **Nightmares:** The loss of a mother is deeply traumatizing, which will manifest itself in nightmares.

c. **Crying:** This is natural, but there may be times the crying seems almost excessive, and it will go on longer than you may think is normal.

d. **Loss of appetite:** Grief can cause a lot of things, and a loss of appetite is one of them. Children will not want to eat, often because they are feeling sorry for themselves, or simply because the grief masks their appetites.

3.   Personalities may completely change, as well. In girls, there may be a complete loss of care for dressing themselves up or for wearing makeup. They could also go the other way and dress more provocatively. There is no way to know which will happen, or if any will happen. For boys, as well as girls, slipping grades, skipped classes, and aggression may come out in school and with you.

4.   The children may build areas of remembrance that include things the mother may have used or owned. Your children may also write notes to her, frame pictures of her,

and talk about her constantly in an effort to remind you that she was there, or to feel that she is there with them at that moment.

5. Do not hide death from your children. Allow them to talk about it with you. They will have a lot of questions about it and while it may be painful to talk about it, it is important in the grieving process.

Depression in the children

When the children lose their mother, depression may seem normal. It is important to distinguish between sadness and depression. Being sad about something is normal, and being sad about losing a mother is expected. Depression comes from sadness. Depression does not fade like sadness does; instead, it grows and lingers. It can interfere with life and make it difficult to manage. In extreme cases, depression leads to suicide. This is why it is important to watch for signs of depression in the children and to help them get through it. In fact, a study done by the University of Pittsburgh found that a parent's death quadruples the risk of depression in children. Roughly 2 percent of children whose parents are both alive will suffer depression, but 10 percent of children who have lost a parent through death suffer depression.

The symptoms described here will be present in children several months after the death of their mothers. In the same University of Pittsburgh study, it was found that the grieving and behavior of the child is heavily influenced by the surviving parent for the first nine months following the death of his or her mother or father. This means that that how you act and deal with the death will influence how your children act and deal with the death. If you are angry, they will become angry. If you are withdrawn, your children will become withdrawn.

If you find that these symptoms continue, it could be a sign that the child is suffering from severe depression.

- Vague complaints of physical problems, including:

    o   Headaches

    o   Stomach aches

    o   Fatigue

    o   Muscle aches

- Skipping of school or slipping grades in school

- Running away from home or threatening to run away from home

- Shouting outbursts

- Irritability for no apparent reason

- Crying for no reason

- Boredom with activities he or she enjoyed in the past

- A loss of friends due to a lack of interest in playing with them

- Substance abuse in teenagers

- A withdrawal away from everyone, or a desire to be isolated

- Poor communication

- A fear of death

- An extreme feeling of fear over failure or being rejected

- Increased anger toward you and others

- Reckless or dangerous behavior, especially in teen males

Talking with teachers and coaches about the children

As a single father, you will only see your children in the evening and the weekends, but there is a large portion of the day when you will not see them: when they are at school. Your children may hide their depression from you, but it is harder to hide it at school. Teachers will be able to see the change in the child's grades, interaction with classmates, and more. This is why it is very important that you talk to your child's teachers and coaches.

When your children go back to school following the death of your wife, you should schedule a meeting with your childrens' teachers to not only explain the circumstances to the teacher, but also to get the teacher's help. You should talk about:

1. The fact that your children have just lost their mother.

2. Signs of depression in your child at school.

3. Changes in behavior of your child in school.

Teachers are a great resource because they are often highly trusted by students, especially in elementary schools. The child may be more open to talk to a teacher than you. It is not because they do not want to talk to you, but simply that they do not know how to talk to you about death, or are worried about upsetting you.

There are some things teachers will be able to watch for and talk to you about:

1. The children are not focusing on school. Your children may have problems concentrating because they are not sleeping well. You can talk with your children and help them get better sleep by addressing their concerns and by being a sounding board for their grief.

2. Class work may not be done because your child has very little interest, or they are stressed. Your children will not complete assignments and may have a general disinterest in anything to do with their class work.

3. Since your children are not sleeping well, are depressed, and are stressed, they will have trouble getting up early in the morning for school. They will want to avoid it. This is something you can talk to the teachers about and the two of you may be able to find solutions.

4. If your children are depressed at school, they will often isolate themselves. Some children have difficulty understanding the emotions they are going through and may feel there is something wrong with them. The problem is that your children need their friends as much as they need you to help them through the depression of losing a mother.

Helping the children grieve and move on

When there has been the death of a parent, it is essential that you help your children with the grieving process so they can make a healthy adjustment to the loss. In order to help your children, there are five things you need to explain to them.

1. Everything is going to die. It is important to show your
    children that everything and everyone will eventually
    die and that it is a natural process. Leaves die in the fall,
    plants die when not watered, and animals die after sev-
    eral years of life. If the children are young enough, they
    may not understand the concept of death, or why their
    mother has left. This is why it is an important concept to
    teach them. Of course, that does not mean you should not
    explain to them that while everything dies, everything
    has a chance to live. Explain to them the importance of
    appreciating life for what a wonderful gift that it is. Only
    focusing on the death aspect could scare your children if
    you are not careful.

2. Your children will probably ask you "What is death?"
    This can be hard to answer. You can go for the technical
    answer and say, "The absence of life," but that will not
    help your children. Instead, explain that sometimes,
    through accidents, disease, and old age, the body simply
    does not work anymore. You can tell your children that
    death happens and it is not only remembering the loss of
    a loved one, but celebrating the happy memories we have
    with them. Talk to them in ways they can understand.

3. Your children will probably ask you why their mom had
    to die. This is a much harder question to answer. You need
    to tell them that sometimes, things happen that cause
    death. You should explain that it is not their fault, and
    they should not feel guilty about anything. Death can
    happen through accidents and disease. Tell your children
    that as time goes on, and as people get older, death can
    come. If you have lost your own parents, explain to them

the same thing happened to you. If they can relate to you through the loss of a parent, it will help them come to terms with the death.

4. Whatever you happen to believe happens after death, explain that to your children. Tell them death is not the end, but simply a new beginning. Whether it is going to heaven or a spiritual transformation of the soul, they will be able to grieve easier by learning their mother is alive in the afterlife. If you believe it, you can tell your children that eventually all of you will be reunited with each other.

5. Finally, reassure your children. Tell them that just because their mother has died, that does not mean you are going to die anytime soon. Tell your children that you will be there for them always, and if they need to talk about death or want to work through the grief, they only need to come to you. Reassure them that you also feel sad about their mother's death and that grieving together can make it much easier.

DEPRESSION IN YOU

All this talk about helping your children with the depression of losing their mother is important, but what about you? You are going to feel sad, depressed, and you will want to feel better, so what can you do? First, you should look for the signs of complicated grief that can manifest into depression. These include:

- Frequent nightmares
- Withdrawal from social settings
- A constant yearning for your spouse

Typically, complicated grief will come about when there has been a suicide or a traumatic death. You should also look at the difference between being sad and being depressed. It can be hard to know the difference, but if you feel the following, then you may be suffering depression:

- A constant feeling of being worthless
- A constant feeling of hopelessness
- Thoughts of death
- Suicidal thoughts
- Uncontrolled crying
- Delusions
- Slowed physical response
- Slowed thinking response

The chances are good that you will go through depression. Roughly 50 percent of widows and widowers experience depression in the year that follows their spouse's death, according to the Harvard Medical School.

Dealing with the depression

There are things you can do to deal with the depression that you are feeling. It is very important to remember that the image you project to your children will be mirrored by them. Look at these options for dealing with depression:

1. Group support is incredibly important. While your friends and family may be there to help, they may not fully understand what you are going through. This is why it is important that you look for support groups that

can help you because the people in the groups have gone through the same thing as you. Support groups for widows and widowers are found in many varieties, including those that are general and those that are more geared for a certain type of death or illness. Here is a list of support groups that you can contact to find out if there is a group in your area:

a. American Association of Retired Persons: This group has a grief course, bereavement support groups, and one-to-one peer outreach. **www.aarp.org/family/**

b. GriefNet.org: This is a community on the Internet for dealing with grief and loss. These groups are run by e-mail, and they work by linking individuals who have suffered the loss of a spouse, while also serving as a resource for questions. **www.griefnet.org**

c. The National Hospice Foundation: This is an organization that provides bereavement care in communities; your spouse did not have to be part of a hospice program in order for you to take part. **http://www. caringinfo.org/GrievingALoss**

d. National Organization for Victim Assistance: This is a counseling group for victims and survivors of violent crime and disaster. It is a good group if your spouse was murdered and you are looking for people who can relate to your situation. **www.trynova.org/**

e. Society of Military Widows: If your spouse was in the military and was killed in action, you can get guidance

and support from this organization.
www.militarywidows.org/

f. American Association of Suicidology: This group offers lists of support groups meant for survivors of suicide victims. **www.suicidology.com**

g. The National Suicide Prevention Lifeline: This organization also has myriad resource for people who are suffering from suicidal thoughts and for people who think their loved ones are suffering from depression. Visit **www.suicidepreventionlifeline.org/** or call 1-800-273-TALK.

h. Mothers Against Drunk Driving: If you lost your loved one in a motor vehicle accident that could be classified as vehicular homicide, then MADD will provide you with contacts to support groups where you can talk with other widowers about your situation. **www.madd.com**

2. You can also get individual therapy if you do not want to sit in a group and share your thoughts and worries with others. In this case, you should see a counselor or a therapist. They will be able to talk with you one-on-one and help you through any anger or guilt that you may be feeling over the loss of your spouse. Most health insurance providers will cover counseling, especially if you are depressed, abused, or have problems with drugs or alcohol. Call your health insurance provider and ask about the payment options. In some cases, you will be responsible for a co-pay (typically between $10 and $75), or you will be responsible for a deductible. The deductible

means you have to spend a certain amount (sometimes up to $5,000) on counseling before insurance will pay for a specified amount.

3.   Take your time and allow the grief to fade. Some people do not want to talk, and there is nothing wrong with that. In a study done by the Journal of Consulting and Clinical Psychology, widows and widowers who did not want to talk about the loss were followed for two years. It was found that neither talking with others nor writing down their feelings reduced the distress of the loss.

4.   Many people or therapists will suggest writing in a journal to help work through your depression. In your journal, you can write about your feelings and no one will have to hear about your emotions if you would like to keep them private. Try to write in your journal on a regular basis and determine whether it helps you through your grief or depression. Find writing prompts online at Web sites such as Creativity-Portal, at **www.creativity-portal.com**, or start a blog (WordPress works well, at **http://wordpress.com**) and find a creative writing topic. This can also be a good tool for your children to work through their depression or grief.

5.   Find activities to help take your mind off your grief or depression. This can be a course at a local community college (such as ceramics, multimedia design, or business); exercising (such as running, bicycling, or weight lifting); a study group at a church or synagogue; or a hobby club (such as sports fans or a cooking club). You can do some of these activities alone, but you should also find some that incorporate your children.

DEALING WITH THE THREE A'S OF GRIEF

When you lose a loved one, especially a wife, a range of emotions can bubble to the surface. There are three primary emotions that a widower will feel — the three A's. They are anger, abandonment, and absentmindedness.

Anger

It seems odd, but you could feel anger at your spouse for dying. Her death left you with children to raise on your own, and you will be angry at whatever religious icon you believe in for taking your spouse. You may just be angry at the universe itself, but you will be looking for someone to blame. When you are angry, keep it in control. Do not get angry at the children, coworkers, friends, or family. Do not let anger get the better of your life — find ways to control it. Praying will work for some, as will meditation. Forgiving your partner for passing can also help the anger disappear and assist in the moving on part of grief.

Abandonment

Your partner died, and that can lead to feelings of abandonment, no different than the kids feel. There will be an overwhelming feeling of loneliness that consumes your life. Feelings of fear and worry will often come up as you realize that you are going it alone, figuratively speaking, as you have the support of friends and family.

Absentmindedness

Grief can overwhelm a person's mind. It can cause someone to think of only the person who died. If you go through losing a wife, you may find that you are not able to concentrate as much as you once did. You may not hear kids asking you questions. You may have trouble concentrating on something as simple as cooking dinner. This can be dangerous if you work in a high-risk job like construction, or if you are driving to work. Thankfully, it will pass, and being aware of the absentmindedness will also make it easier to manage.

CHAPTER CONCLUSION

Possibly the only thing worse than going through a divorce for a father is dealing with the death of a wife. There are many widowed fathers out there who envy divorced fathers because they at least can still talk to the person who they were once married to. A widowed father does not have that luxury.

The death of a spouse is difficult to deal with, and many husbands think the grief will never leave and their lives will never be the same again. It is true that their lives are changed forever, but the grief will eventually fade. It will always be there, sometimes coming up when least expected, usually during a memory, but it will be manageable.

There can be a great deal of fear when a husband loses his wife in an accident or through an illness. He is now a single father, raising one or more children on his own. He wonders if he will be able to handle his own grief, as well as the grief of his children. He may think that he is not up to the task and a feeling of running from it all will rise.

As a father, you need to be there for your children to help them manage their grief, while you manage your own. It may not be easy; however, once the grief passes, you and your children will feel closer. You will have a relationship with them that you never thought possible.

"It is a wise father that knows his own child. "

— William Shakespeare, English playwright

2

Balancing Life

"Blessed indeed is the man who hears
many gentle voices call him father!"
— Lydia Maria Child, American
abolitionist and women's rights activist

Facing Your Job As A Single Parent

> *"Nothing I've ever done has given me more joys*
> *and rewards than being a father to my children."*
>
> — Bill Cosby, author, comedian, and actor

There is a difference between being a father with a partner and being a single father in terms of how you deal with work. When you have help being a father, you can balance work and fatherhood much easier. However, when you are a single father, the duties are all on you when the children stay at your place, and that means a new balance at work needs to be created.

CHANGING YOUR SCHEDULE

Having a more flexible schedule is important, especially if you only see the children every Wednesday night and every other weekend. With a flexible work week, you can make the most of the time you have with your children. Unless you are self-employed, you may have to talk to your employer about changing the work schedule. This can go either way. Some bosses will be more than happy to help you out, while others will feel that you were a father before the divorce and you managed just fine then.

Thankfully, there are several ways to change your schedule so that you work the same but have more time for your children. Try these tips:

- When the kids are not visiting you, work extra hours. For example, if you see the kids Wednesday night, Friday night, all of Saturday, and part of Sunday, then you will adjust your schedule on Wednesday and Friday to make the most of your time with them. If they get out of school at 3 p.m., plan to leave at that time on Wednesdays and Fridays instead of 5:30 p.m. — that is five extra hours each week with your kids. On the weeks that you do not see your kids, work an extra five hours to make up for leaving early the weeks you do see your kids.

- If you cannot work extra time due to company policy, then try and adjust the time that you work on days you see your kids. Work from 6:30 a.m. to 2:30 p.m. instead of 9 a.m. to 5 p.m. on days you see your children. Usually, most bosses will be happy with this arrangement.

- Look at job sharing with someone else or working part-time. This way, you can cut back on your hours, while spending time with your children. The only obvious problem is making less money. If you are paying child support, that may be an issue.

- Talk to your boss about not being an employee, but being a consultant or contractor. Companies like this because they do not have to pay as much in health benefits and you will like it because you can charge more as a contractor, while at the same time making your own hours.

TELECOMMUTING

One great option that many single fathers use is telecommuting, or working from home. With the Internet, this is more common than ever before. When you telecommute, you can make your own hours and spend time with your children while you are working. It is a great option that many single fathers want to take advantage of. To work from home, you will need:

- A work computer
- A separate phone line
- A fax machine
- Access to the Internet
- An office setting in your home

Naturally, there are some jobs that are more suited to working from home than others. You can conduct data entry from home with company program software, but you cannot work at a construction site or be a police officer from home. If your job is suited for working from home, talk to your boss about the possibility. Another benefit of working from home is you will not pay for parking and you will save on gas. That means more money for the kids, or to pay child support.

WHAT HAPPENS WITH A POOR WORK-LIFE BALANCE

If, for whatever reason, you find that you cannot strike a good work-life balance, your relationship with your children will change. Whether it is because your boss will not give you the time or your job just does not lend itself to flexibility in hours, how you react is generally the same.

Guilt will be a common emotion in this circumstance because you cannot spend as much time with your children as you would like. Ironically, these feelings of guilt can cause a father to distance himself from the children to keep the guilt away, too. The best way to deal with this guilt is to make the most of the time when you are with your children. Do not get involved in your own things and do not answer the phone — just concentrate on them.

The other problem with having a poor work-life balance is that you can overcompensate to make up for the lost time. In contrast to not giving enough time, when you overcompensate, you can seem over controlling to your children because you demand all their time to make up for the time you spent at work.

TALKING WITH THE BOSS

Generally, people will spend 40 hours per week at work, which amounts to about 2,000 hours per year (if you subtract two weeks of standard paid vacation). That is a large portion of life spent working, and that means that some people see their boss more than the family. The boss can be a friend or an irritation, but he or she is a part of a single father's life. A single father needs three people following a divorce or widowhood: his kids, his best friend, and his boss.

Whether you want to or not, the personal issues from your changed life will follow you to work. When those issues make their way into work, your supervisors and bosses will see them and will have to deal with those issues. When a man goes through a divorce or widowhood, there is a change in his work behavior. Productivity goes down as his mind is filled with the emotions of loss, worry, and anger that come with suddenly being a single father. This is why it is so important to talk to one's boss about the changed situation.

If you were able to make $4,000 in commission every month on your sales, then it can be expected that immediately after the divorce or widowhood, your sales may drop to $2,000. An employer is going to notice this. If a salesman's commission is 10 percent of a sale, it amounts to $20,000 of lost income that week for the company. Your boss is going to want to know why you did not bring in your usual sales. He or she may think that it was because of poor time management or a disinterest in doing well. You may find that your job is threatened. The only way to make your boss understand is to tell him or her about the changing situation and how you are now a single father. By talking to your boss, you can make him or her see it from your point of view. If your boss is also a single parent, you are in a great situation because your boss will know exactly what you are going through.

It is very important to show your boss the new pressures that you are juggling at that moment. You may arrive late some days, or need to leave early to pick up the children. There also may be days you do not want to work. How productive will you be on a day when your kids are sitting at home with a baby-sitter while you are working in an office? It is impossible for your mind to stay on your work in that type of situation.

It is important to talk with your boss and tell him or her that you will be working harder than before to make up for the changing schedule. Be honest with your boss; explain how your life has changed and talk about the new pressures that have fallen on you.

Explain to your boss these three important points:

1. Creative ways for you to do your work more productively

2. The value you give to your boss

3.   How you can manage your career and your role as a single father

How to talk to the boss

Schedule a meeting with your boss and follow these tips to ensure that it goes well for you:

- Be positive and make sure you smile when you are talking to your boss. Going into his or her office with a frown or a belief that you have to be aggressive to get what you want will not go well for you.

- Be polite and respectful with your boss. He or she may have gone through the same situation as you, and being respectful to your boss and his or her own knowledge on the subject can help.

- If you need to take a day off, be sure you give your boss plenty of notice. Do not ask for the day off the day before. Your boss may need to find someone to cover for you, and if you give plenty of notice, it is easier for him or her to do so.

- Do not use confrontational words when asking to have a more flexible schedule.

- Use the word "I" instead of using "you." For example: "I think that I will be able to generate increased productivity if I change my work hours to manage my new single father role better." An example of how not to word requests: "You will find that by changing the schedule, your sector's productivity will increase. This is something that you need to do to ensure that company profits do not fall."

- Be careful of your body language. Body language makes up about 75 percent of your communication by some estimates, so you can say a lot just by how you stand. Do not cross your arms because it can be construed as confrontational. Also, do not point your finger, and do not stand over your boss. Sit in a relaxed manner with open arms to show you have nothing to hide.

- Do not focus on the negatives; only focus on the positives. For example, do not start by saying, "Being a single dad has caused my schedule to change, and if I cannot change my work schedule, I do not know if I can stay working here." Instead, say, "Now that I am a single father, things have changed for me. However, I think it is possible to manage these changes efficiently by changing my hours to be more flexible. In my proposal, I work the same hours, but I work them in a more flexible manner, with some hours from home." *An example of a proposal is included in the Appendix.*

- Get straight to the point. Tell your boss about the issue and what you would like in a clear and concise manner. The more you dance around the issue, the harder it will be to ask for what you want and get your boss to listen to you. He or she is busy and made time for you, so do not waste that time.

- When you talk to your boss, do not talk to him or her during lunch or at a busy time of day. Make sure you do not talk to your boss in front of other coworkers, either.

Your boss may feel pressured by the coworkers to agree to what you are asking for, or your boss may be angry that you are bringing up this issue in front of others because it is a personal matter.

- Always end on a positive note. Thank your boss for listening to you and let him or her know that whatever is decided, having a job where your boss hears your concerns and knows what is going on in your life makes everything easier.

REQUESTING TIME OFF AFTER A DIVORCE

Taking time off following a divorce can be very important. There has been a large change in your life and there needs to be time to adjust to that. As a result, taking time off can be a beneficial idea. It allows you to meet the change in your life head-on.

Time off allows you to do a number of things:

1. Spend time with your kids, helping them get used to the changing family dynamic.

2. Spend time alone to help you adjust to the new situation in your life.

3. Help find balance in your life and prepare you for the road ahead as a single father.

REQUESTING TIME OFF AFTER THE DEATH OF A SPOUSE

Companies are often very aware of how difficult it can be to concentrate on work following a divorce. As a result, companies will often do a wide variety of things to help after you lose your spouse, than if you are divorced.

Most companies will have written policies that dictate how much time off employees can have after a death in a family. Some policies will depend more on the situation and which family member died. When there has been a death of a spouse, companies will often send flowers to the funeral and a company representative will also show up at the funeral to show support. It should be noted that under the Family and Medical Leave Act, leave for the death of a family member is not covered. In order to qualify, you need to show that the bereavement is causing a health problem in you, including depression. It can also apply if your children are suffering health problems because of the death of your spouse. Visit **www.dol.gov/whd/fmla/index.htm/** for more information on updates to the act.

You should talk to your superiors about bereavement or funeral leave. This type of leave is time off that is given to you by your employer to settle matters relating to the funeral and the will. Generally, the time you get off for bereavement will be a few days, but with good companies, you can get several weeks off. There is no legal obligation for an employer to pay you during bereavement leave, but he or she is not allowed to fire you for being away from work during that leave. Some companies will consider bereavement leave to be personal time off, sick days, or vacation time, and not something separate. California, for example, has a policy that gives paid time off to employees so they can arrange, plan, and attend the funeral of a loved one. Sadly, many companies will expect the employee to get his mind back on work and get over the grief, even if it was a spouse who died, once the funeral leave has been used.

USING VACATION AND SICK DAYS

One option at your disposal is to use your sick days and vacation days. That way, you can still be paid. The problem with using sick days is that you may need proof from a doctor, so using vacation days is a much better option. While you probably had a better plan in mind for your vacation days, taking time off work to deal with being a single father is important, and so is being paid. You need to keep money coming in to your bank account, especially if you are paying child support, so taking vacation days allows you to do that. Also, your employer does not care how employees use vacation days or what they do during them. Therefore, you do not have to explain anything to your bosses if you do not want to about the divorce or the death of a spouse. Some companies require their employees to use their vacation days each year, rather than allow them to pile up over the years, so this is your best chance to use those days. Generally, you should get two to three weeks of vacation, and that time can be used to help you create balance in your new life.

REQUESTING A LEAVE OF ABSENCE

Requesting a leave of absence from work can help you deal with the issues in your life, and can help you connect with your children on a single father level. A leave of absence can be quite a bit longer than your vacation days, giving you more time to adjust. A leave of absence is defined as a period of time where an individual is away from his job, but is still an employee of the company. There are two types of leave of absences: paid and unpaid.

Paid leaves are usually suggested by the employer, rather than the employee. Typically, a paid leave comes about due to an injury, repairs in the building, bereavement, or jury duty. Unpaid leave is much more common and comes about as a request from the employee rather than the employer. There can be many different reasons for unpaid leave, including dealing with death or divorce. An employer does not have to allow an employee to go on an unpaid leave of absence, but the Family and Medical Leave Act of 1993 requires companies to grant unpaid leave in certain circumstances. These circumstances are:

1. The birth of a child, an adoption, or the placement of a child in foster care with the employee

2. To care for a spouse, parent, or child who has a serious medical problem

3. If a serious health problem is preventing the employee from being able to work

To qualify for the FMLA, an employee must also meet the following criteria:

1. Employed for the last 12 months

2. Worked at least 1,250 hours in the last 12 months

3. The company the employee works for has 50 or more employees working within 75 miles

Chances are, you will not be approved for an unpaid leave of absence through the FMLA. That does not mean you will not get your leave of absence from your employer. Because taking time off due to divorce is not covered under the FMLA, there is no obligation by the employer to grant it and you may be out of a job if you do take a leave of absence. If you have suffered the death of a spouse, you will probably be offered an unpaid leave of absence. In fact, you may get a paid leave of absence if you are a new widower with children.

If you do take a leave of absence that is unpaid, which the employer grants, there are ways to still make income. The most common is to draw money from your retirement plan. If you do this and you are under the age of 59.5 years, then you will have to pay a 10 percent penalty on withdrawals under IRS law. This means that if you take out $20,000, then you will have to pay $2,000 for the penalty.

If you do end up taking a leave of absence, there are a few things you can do to make the entire process easier on your coworkers, your boss, and yourself.

- It is important to notify your employer as soon as you can. This will allow your boss to fill the position with a temporary employee while you are away.

- Give your employer all the information he or she will need about your leave of absence, including why you are going, how long you will be gone, and whether or not you will return.

- Work with your coworkers and replacement by offering to answer any questions they may have about your duties.

- Leave on good terms for your leave of absence. You may be coming back, but even if you are not, always be gracious when you walk out for possibly the last time.

When you return from your leave of absence, show your appreciation to those people who took over from you. Often, coworkers will shoulder the load of an employee who is gone, which can mean extra work. A token of gratitude, whether a lunch, note, or a small gift, can go a long way to helping mend any hard feelings that your coworkers may have about doing your job while you were gone.

When you come back from your leave of absence, be sure you put together all your child care arrangements while on leave. That way, when you return to work, determining who will take care of your children is not something you have to worry about.

WHAT TO DO ON YOUR LEAVE OF ABSENCE

Once you have your leave of absence, you may not want to sit around thinking about the fact that you are now a single parent. Instead, you may want to get your mind off it and get down to work. You may also want to make money. With your leave of absence, you can leave the pressure of work, while getting your mind off your troubles.

- If there is anything around the house that needs to be taken care of, now would be a good time to deal with it. Whether that means repairing plumbing problems, fixing the roof, or just doing landscaping, handyman work can be a great way to get your mind off of everything and keep yourself busy.

- With this time off, spend as much time with the kids as you can. If you have partial custody, at least some of the time off during your leave of absence can be spent with the kids. It is important that you take this time because it shows your kids that you want to stay a part of their lives and you want to do things with them, even at the expense of work. Go out with them and have fun — it is a great way to get yourself grounded on your leave of absence.

- You can also look for some ways to pay the bills while you are not at work. You can do handy work for friends and others in your community, but you can also work out of your home. There are several Web sites that cater to helping people work from home:

  o Guru (**www.guru.com**): This is the largest and most famous freelancing Web site. This site contracts people for jobs in various fields, including writing, design, accounting, and data entry find work. You can register for a basic, free account or pay up to $200 for more tailored results. While signing up, Guru will walk you through categories and you can begin searching for projects that match your skill set. Free skill tests, a tailored profile, and your resume will be able to show companies your qualifications. There are individuals who make a lot of money working on these projects, and some work completely from home.

  o ELance (**www.elance.com**): Like Guru, this freelancing Web site helps individuals find the work they are looking for to make money. If you are on a leave of absence, this would be a good Web site to join, as it can bring in a lot of work. It is also a good complement to Guru for extra work.

  o Craigslist (**www.craigslist.com**): If you live in an urban area, you can advertise your services on Craigslist. It is free and you can potentially reach thousands of people in your area. Some call it the classified ads of the Internet, and for good reason.

If you do not want to put any information online because you worry about your bosses seeing it and letting you go because they think you are trying to find other work, you can advertise in your own area for something not relating to your job. Put up fliers advertising that you can do handyman work or yard work. Try to choose work that does not interfere with your full-time job. For example, if you are a technical writer at your work, your bosses may frown on you doing contract technical work.

- Take a trip and clear your head. Being away from your troubles can be a great way to relax. If you do not have much money, that does not mean you cannot take a short vacation. Simply go to a neighboring town and stay in a hotel. If you enjoy being outdoors, take two weeks and go for a long hike in the wilderness. This can be an amazing way to center yourself and help you get back to who you are. Obviously, this solution does not always work depending on your circumstances. If you are a widower, you need to take care of your children, but that does not mean you cannot take them with you. Spending time together following the death of their mother can help both you and them get closer and deal with your grief. If you are divorced, you will probably be able to go away. You can also try the concept of a "staycation," which is simply staying home but isolating yourself from everything for a few days so you can get grounded once again.

CHAPTER CONCLUSION

One of the biggest adjustments that a new single father has to go through is trying to determine how work is going to fit into his new life. When he was married, a father could count on his wife to help shoulder the load, or at least help out so that it all was not on the father. However, through divorce or widowhood, there may not be any help now, and the time a father spends with his children seems all the more precious.

For that reason, it is important for a father to find ways to get work to accommodate the new reality of his life. Whether it is taking time off from work, adjusting a schedule, or working from home, there are many alternatives available for a father who has to juggle work and children and achieve a new work-life balance.

6 Child Care

> *"My father gave me the greatest gift anyone could*
> *give another person, he believed in me."*
>
> — Jim Valvano, NCAA champion college basketball coach

E
ven if you are able to strike a good work-life balance, there will be times you need someone to take care of your younger children. It may be because of working late, or perhaps you are not able to take a particular day off. When this happens, you need child care. For a father, child care is often a difficult subject. Whether through divorce or widowhood, a single father is protective of his children and worries about anyone else watching them. Whether a father wants someone else watching his children or not, there will be times when it is needed.

WHERE TO FIND CHILD CARE

There are several avenues that you can use to find someone to watch your children while you are away. Look at these possibilities to find a baby-sitter who will work best for you and your children.

- **Friends:** You trust your friends and know them well. Not only could they be a good resource as someone who can watch the children, but they may also know a baby-sitter they can recommend to you. Your friends may not have time to baby-sit since they have careers of their own, but if they know an individual involved with child care, it can make your entire search much easier.

- **Newspaper advertisements:** One ad in a newspaper that states you are looking for a baby-sitter, what you pay, and the hours you need the baby-sitter can help you in your effort to find someone competent to watch your children. One newspaper ad could end up bringing you dozens of applicants, allowing you to pick the best one for the job.

- **Baby-sitter agencies:** Depending on where you live, there will be agencies that contract out baby-sitters. These agencies have very high standards for their baby-sitters and they all go through a rigorous application process. Finding a baby-sitter this way costs more, but you are paying for the peace of mind knowing your children are safe.

- **Day cares:** Instead of having someone come to your home, you can take your children to a day care or child care center. Day cares cost between $80 and $400 per week, depending on where you live and the size of the day care. That higher cost comes with the fact that you know your children are being watched in a safe setting. This option generally only works for younger children. Your 10-year-old may not want to spend his or her afternoons hanging around a bunch of 4-year-olds.

Web sites to find nannies and baby-sitters

If you are looking for a baby-sitter or nanny in your area and you want to use the Internet to find them, you are in luck. There are several excellent baby-sitter and nanny Web sites that can help you find the person who will make your life easier.

- **Sitter City (www.sittercity.com)**: This Web site is the largest and most trusted of all the sitter/nanny Web sites. In addition, it also provides elderly care givers, tutors, and dog sitters/walkers. Started in 2001, there are now more than one million caregivers listed on the Web site, based out of almost every city in the United States. The site allows you to post a job that lists what you need, and qualified sitters will then contact you. You can search for the baby-sitter/nanny that you want based on 50 different criteria. You can also look at pictures, experience, and qualifications of the sitters. In addition, you can read their reviews, background checks (this costs the caregiver $10), and references (provided by the caregiver). The Internet is free to use.

- **Phone A Babysitter (www.phoneababysitter.com)**: This Web site provides baby-sitters for parents in both the United States and Canada. Currently, 32,000 baby-sitters are listed on the Web site, all of which are searchable based on your location. Parents can look through the profiles of the sitters, learn about their experience, and contact their references. This is one of the cheapest baby-sitter sites, offering lifetime memberships for $29.99.

- **Care.com (www.care.com)**: This is another large baby-sitter Web site that has thousands of profiles listed. You can search for a nanny or sitter based on your location. You are provided with a list of the baby-sitters, and then you can view the profile of each. At this point, you can check references, ratings, and reviews, as well as get free background checks on the baby-sitters. While the Web site offers a free basic membership, this membership only gives you limited access to sitters. To have unlimited access and free background checks, you need to sign up for a paying account. Care.com has higher costs than other nanny and sitter Web site. For one month, it is $30; for three months, it is $60; and for 12 months, it is $120.

- **Great Au Pair (www.greataupair.com)**: If you are looking for a nanny, this is the site to visit. Available worldwide, it has tens of thousands of profiles listed. Since 2001, it has been providing baby-sitters and nannies to customers around the globe. With Great Au Pair, you register for free and create a family profile. Nannies can then find you and contact you with their credentials and information. Memberships can be purchased on a 90-day or 30-day basis. The 90-day membership costs $120, and the 30-day membership costs $60. You can also maintain a free account, but you will have limited access to certain information.

- **Online-Nanny (www.online-nanny.com)**: This is the sister site of Sitter City and runs on the same principle of searching for a nanny and hiring him or her. You can look at references and even do background checks on the nannies. The service is available across the United States, as well as in Canada. The costs for this Web site are the same as the costs for Sitter City.

LOOKING FOR DAY CARE CLUES

If you do decide to take your children to day care, or to a child care center, there are things you can look for to ensure that your children are going to be safe in this new environment. It is not an easy task to leave children with someone else in a strange setting. Looking for clues as to the quality of the care can help put your mind at ease. Here are some of the things to look for:

- Look at the children's area and make sure it is clean and safe. If it is a little dirty, it does not necessarily mean that the place is bad for your child. If there are 20 children running around at the time, it would be impossible for the center not to be a bit dirty.

- The gate to the center should lock firmly.

- The staff of the day care/child care center should be qualified, and each should have training in children's CPR and first aid.

- The kids should have enough toys to keep them busy.

- For the children who like to read, there should be plenty of books to keep them interested.

- Ask about the playtime activities and what is scheduled for the day. This way, you can know what your kids will be doing while you are away at work.

- Find out what kind of food the children will be fed during the day to ensure your children get something healthy to eat.

- Find out the policy on children being picked up, and how the day care/child care center ensures that only the right people pick up a child.

- Trust your instincts. If you have a bad feeling about the place, do not enroll your child in the day care/child care center.

What to avoid when choosing a child care center

Looking for certain things in the child care center is important because you want to know as much about the place your children will be when you are away as you can. Therefore, it is important you choose the right place for yourself and your children. Below are several tips to help you choose the best child care center option for your children.

1. Do not choose a child care center based only on its location. It is important to find a place that is close to your home or work so that you do not have to travel far to pick up the kids. However, if you are only choosing a child care center based on its location, your options become severely limited. Location is not the only consideration when choosing a center. Qualifications like education, environment, hours, safety, and staff expertise are all important.

2. There is a belief that the more you spend on child care, the better it will be. There are many parents who choose a child care center because of its prestige, but just because a center has prestige does not mean that it is going to be the right location for your children. There are some child care centers that are so exclusive, parents make reservations

for their children before they are even born. Even if your friends say this is the best child care center for your child, that does not mean it is true. The best child care is the one that works for both you and your children.

3.   As a single father, you can be excused for trying to save money. You probably will not be putting your children in the high-cost prestigious child care program, but you do not want to put your children in a bargain child care center, either. Cheap child care can be hard not to overlook because of your finances, but remember: You get what you pay for. If they do not charge much, there may be a reason for that.

4.   There is nothing wrong with trusting the recommendation of a friend with a child care center, but that should not be your only criterion. Take your friend's advice and look at the child care center, but make your own judgment. If the place does not feel right, do not go with it, despite what your friend says about it.

5.   Never go into a child care center decision without first doing research. It is important to know everything about the child care center before your children are sent there. Do not be afraid of finding out every detail about the center. If a child care center is not willing to give good answers to your questions, find another place for your children.

6.   If you are afraid there is no one better than your current child care center, you will not look for another center. Sure, there is a chance that the next child care center you take your kids to is going to be worse, but there is just as

much reason to say that it will be better, as well. If you have concerns that you voice to the owners of the child care center, and those concerns are not addressed, just take the risk. You want the best for your children, which means you may have to go through a few child care providers before you find the best one.

CHOOSING A BABY-SITTER

If you decide to have someone watch the children in your own home where your children are more comfortable, you are going to need to hire a baby-sitter. Baby-sitters are easy to find. The important thing is finding one you are comfortable with and who you know your children will be safe with. There are several things that need to be done during the process of choosing a sitter, all of which will be covered in this section. In regards to whether or not your children need a sitter, if they are younger than nine years old, they will need one. If they are 10 or older, they can be left alone for longer and may not need a sitter.

Some Questions To Ask

When you begin to interview a baby-sitter, go through these questions. Ask the ones most relevant to you and your children to ensure that you learn as much as you can from the sitter so you can make a reliable decision. Underneath certain questions is how you will want the baby-sitter to answer.

1. **What is your experience with baby-sitting?** Generally you will want the baby-sitter to have one or more years of experience, and experience with the age group of children that your kids fall into. Experience can come from having

siblings, from being a camp counselor, from random baby-sitting jobs, or from volunteering at elementary schools.

2. **Do you have training in first aid?** It should be noted that you, as the person hiring the sitter, should be the one who pays for the first aid training. If the baby-sitter does not have the training and you want to hire him or her, let the sitter know you will get him or her trained. Contact the American Red Cross at **www.redcross.org** or by telephone at 1-800-REDCROSS.

3. **Do you spend a lot of time with children when you are not baby-sitting?**

4. **Do you have current immunizations?** You will want the baby-sitter to be immunized for the flu and any childhood diseases. If your children get chicken pox and spread it to the baby-sitter, it can cause serious health problems for the sitter.

5. **Are there any health issues that I should be aware of?** You want to make sure that your baby-sitter does not have any health issues that could become a problem if he or she is baby-sitting. These include seizures and diabetes. The last thing you want is to have your children trying to care for the baby-sitter while you are gone.

6. **What games and activities do you have in place for when you are watching my children?** If the baby-sitter does not have any games planned, he or she has not done the homework. You want someone who is going to spend time with your children, not let them sit and watch television.

7. **What ages of children have you baby-sat for before?**
   If the sitter has not baby-sat your children's age group
   before, you should look into finding another person.
   The reason for this is because if he or she is only used to
   baby-sitting 9-year-olds, and you have two 3-year-olds, it
   is going to be a different set of circumstances for them.

8. **If a child is sick, do you know how to administer medication to them?** Like first aid, you want your child to be
   taken care of in case something goes wrong. Providing
   training in regards to medication for your baby-sitter is
   very important.

9. **How will you handle children who are fighting, or
   children who are having separation anxiety?**

10. **If one of the children is not listening to you, how will
    you respond?** You want the baby-sitter to answer in a way
    that shows he or she will have authority in a situation, but
    will not result in the loss of temper. If he or she does not
    have an answer, that could be a problem.

11. **Is there anything I can do to make the work environ-
    ment more welcoming or easier for you?**

12. **What kind of meals will you prepare for the children?**
    This is to make sure that the baby-sitter will prepare
    healthy meals for your children and not just heat up mini-
    pizzas every day. Offer to spend time with the baby-sitter
    to teach him or her how to cook healthy meals. Pay him or
    her for this training time.

13. **If a child begins to start choking, do you know what
    to do?**

14. **How much do you charge per hour?** Generally, the rate will depend on your location, the person's experience, the ages of the children, and the number of children.

15. **What hours are you available to work?**

16. **If you commit to baby-sitting at a certain time, can I rely on you not to cancel unless it is an emergency on your end?**

17. **What do you think makes you a good baby-sitter?** A good sitter is someone who has maturity and judgement and enjoys doing fun things with children. He or she should know about the behaviors of children. In addition, a good baby-sitter should understand dietary needs, as well how to deal with emergencies.

18. **Can you tell me about your worst baby-sitting experience and why that was your worst experience?**

19. **Can you tell me about your best baby-sitting experience and why that was your best experience?**

20. **Do you have references?** Generally, the sitter's references will be teachers, employers for other jobs, parents of children he or she has baby-sat for, or friends and family. Friends and family may be the most honest.

Let the children meet the baby-sitter

Once you have interviewed the baby-sitters and chosen five that are the best of the bunch, you should do a field test with the children. First, let the children meet the sitter. By letting the children meet and be alone with the baby-sitter, you can learn a lot about whether or not the baby-sitter is right for your children. Often, when parents are looking for sitters, they choose one based on what they see, not what they learn from their children. You may rave about a new baby-sitter you are about to hire, but your children may not like the individual at all. Children are perceptive, and they can pick up on things that adults do not.

One thing you can do is a field test by testing how good they are with your children in real-life situations. Have five sitters lined up to baby-sit at different times. Once all five have had a baby-sitting field test, you can talk to your children and find out what they thought. This way, you learn what the baby-sitter does, how the children react to the person, and whether or not the sitter will be a good fit for you and your family. Ask your kids how the baby-sitter interacted with them, if the baby-sitter ever raised his or her voice, and what he or she did in the home while the children were playing. This way, you can learn as much as you need to from your children to make a good decision on which baby-sitter to hire.

Never forget about learning from your own children as to whether a baby-sitter is going to be a good fit for the job or not. By talking to your children, you will find out if the sitter makes your children happier and makes the time you spend apart from them easier.

HIRING A NANNY

If you decide to hire a live-in nanny, you need to ensure you go through the entire hiring process properly. You want to hire someone with whom you are comfortable and who is comfortable with you and your children. Often, hiring a nanny can be more time-intensive than the process of hiring a baby-sitter.

First, you should define your needs to a nanny. Let the nanny know exactly what it is you are looking for. Some things to outline include:

1. Skills you want the nanny to have

2. What you consider to be the ideal nanny

3. Your scheduling needs

4. What you can afford

5. What duties (cooking, cleaning, light housework) you will expect the nanny to perform

To find a nanny, you can go through the Web sites previously mentioned, or you can go through a nanny agency. One consideration for using nanny agencies is that they will take about 10 to 15 percent of the nanny's salary, which may result in the nanny increasing what he or she charges to compensate.

If you go through a Web site, you will get a list of nannies in your area, which you will have to go through to find the nannies who are going to fit your needs. If you go through a nanny agency, it will provide you with pre-screened candidates you can look at. The first interview should be the telephone interview, which is not quite an interview. You will call the nanny to get information, which you can then use to evaluate whether he or she makes the short list. Some things you can ask the nanny over the phone include:

1. When can you start?

2. What hours can you work?

3. What are your salary expectations?

4. Can you drive, and do you hold an up-to-date driver's license?

5. Do you need anything for the job?

You should also tell the nanny about the home, your children, and what ages they are. Anything you can think of to tell the nanny, you should. The nanny may not want to deal with 2-year-olds, so you can eliminate him or her from the short list immediately. After you have done phone interviews, you can schedule in-person interviews with your short list of candidates. You can either schedule the in-person interview in a public place, or you can have the nanny come to your home. If you are not keen on having a stranger in your home, or the nanny does not want to go to your home yet, a neutral place may be the best choice. This in-person interview is important, and you should watch for several cues as to how the nanny will perform with your children. Look for the following:

1. Does the nanny arrive on time?

2. Did he or she follow the directions to get to your home properly?

3. Was the nanny well-dressed and groomed?

4. Did the nanny come with her resume ready to show you?

5. Did he or she seem to be out-going and ready to answer questions?

6. What first impression did the nanny give you?

Instead of an interview where you are simply sitting across from each other, you can also schedule a working interview with the nanny. During the working interview, have the nanny spend a few hours with you and your children in your home. This will allow the nanny to not only become familiar with you and your home, but you can see how he or she responds to situations and how comfortable he or she seems in your home.

Following the interviews, you should check the references of the individuals who have made the short list. References will help you make your decision — look for red flags. If the applicant has no references, he or she should not be hired. Family members of the nanny should not be references, so do not accept them.

Next, perform background checks. To do this, get a signed consent form from each candidate to order a pre-employment background check. On this form, you need:

1.   Any aliases he or she has

2.   Social security number

3.   Where he or she has lived for the past seven years

With the background check, you should look at the driving record, any criminal records from the past seven years, and if he or she is listed on a state sex offender registry.

Next, create a nanny contract. This will be covered in the next section. Following the interviews, background checks, and contract signing, you can get the nanny oriented with where he or she will be working. With the orientation, you will show the nanny your home, introduce him or her to your children if you have not yet, and show him or her the logistics of what he or she will be doing. Orientations can take a few hours to a few days, and it can help you see how your nanny will work with your children and around the house. Show the nanny everything he or she will need to know, including where all the cleaning products are, how the appliances work, and any emergency contact numbers you have listed.

CASE STUDY: SINGLE DAD DISCUSSES DAY CARE AND DISABLED CHILDREN

Craig Haller
Single father * Small business owner
craig@macraigor.com

I have two children, a son and a daughter, both severely disabled. By profession, I am a geek, owning a high-tech company as well as a small, start-up coffee company, which evolved from a love of coffee. My time is obviously consumed by work during the day, and by being the sole care-taker of my teenage daughter in the evenings and the weekends. I have been single for just more than 10 years, and nothing could have prepared me for this roller coaster.

My wife of 10 years announced that she was "not happy" and could not state a reason. After three months of couple's therapy, in which a reason never did emerge, she moved out with my son. After a few years, she was unable to properly care for our son.

Logistically I could not have him live with me and his sister, so he went to a superb residential program. That leaves me and my wonderful daughter, Hannah Pearl, now a teenager — nay, a young woman. Although I am single, there are many wonderful women in our lives, including nannies and ex-nannies.

We adjusted to our new lifestyle rather quickly. Since my daughter has no communication at all, I do not know how she felt about it. In general, she appeared to "go with the flow." I did not have time to worry about my own adjustment. There is too much to do on a daily basis to dawdle.

As a result of our situation, there are many big challenges, and the smaller, typical ones are magnified. In any relationship, it is important to try to understand the other's point of view. I have obviously never been a pre-pubescent young girl, nor a teenage girl. I have also never been non-verbal, non-mobile, or completely unable to communicate. There are many women in our lives who are able to help with some of the situations that typically arise with a teenage daughter (physical changes, social issues), but alas, there are big complications because of her special needs that only I can address. For example, dealing with seizures and emergencies while alone. The normal challenges exist, such as getting child care at non-essential times so I can date or travel, finding some type of female role model for my daughter, and having a partner for myself on this ride of a lifetime.

At times, the issues surrounding child care are a nightmare. I cannot hire a "typical" baby-sitter, such as a high school student, because Hannah at times has needs that require greater level of responsibility. I have help with Hannah when she comes home from school until dinner time, and for a few hours Saturday — that is only time I can do my errands and recharge my manhood at Home Depot. There is no appropriate after-school day care available for my daughter, hence the reliance on nannies. I intentionally do not hire anyone for Sundays, which lets me to do what I want to do — spend a full day with my daughter.

Until very recently, all of the nannies for my children were Russian. The first was Russian by coincidence; then one recommends another, and so on. The interesting part is that they have great backgrounds.

They come here legally with work permits, but often cannot work in their specific field because of licenses and such. I find that there are uncomfortable times when I need to discuss Hannah's "woman's issues" with the nanny, wishing I had a wife to handle those discussions. Here I am, with my stunted Russian, trying to discuss the most intimate subjects when I am not sure I even know all the words in English! It is definitely a challenge when I have my own full-time job, but the benefits are rewarding. We have had several nannies over the years. Most of these women have remained our close friends — our families spend holidays together. Hannah brings new perspectives on the world to them, and they bring wonderful insights and friendship to us.

Creating a work agreement or contract for the nanny

When you hire a nanny, you need to create a work agreement or contract with her that outlines the job, responsibilities, compensation, and benefits. A nanny contract should include the following:

- In the contract, clearly outline when the nanny is expected to work during the week and what hours each day he or she will work. You should also outline the amount of notice time you need in case the nanny has to cancel.

- If the nanny will live with you, the living arrangements will need to be described in the contract. Outline details of the nanny's bedroom, bathroom, privacy, Internet connection, and whether or not food is included. If he or she will be a live-out nanny, this should be addressed in the contract.

- The nanny salary should be outlined in the contract. Include how much and how often he or she will be paid (weekly, bi-weekly, or monthly). In addition, the contract needs to outline how taxes and overtime pay will be handled. According to the International Nanny Association (**www.nanny.org**), nannies with fewer years of experience should make $250 to $400 per week. Professional nannies with years of experience should make between $400 and $1,000 per week.

- Naturally, the duties and responsibilities of the nanny should be in the contract. By listing these terms, you can ensure that you minimize disagreements and disputes in the future.

- In the contract, specify who the nanny should contact in case of an emergency.

- Some nannies may need to drive your children to and from school, home, and extracurricular activities. In the contract, define whether the nanny should use his or her own car or your car, and whether or not he or she will be compensated for gas and mileage. Include a safety statement in the contract that defines seating arrangements for the children in the car and rules that require the nanny to not only wear a seat belt, but to refrain from using a cell phone while driving.

- Any benefits the nanny incurs should be in the contract, including how many personal, sick, and vacation days he or she gets. Typically, nannies get about 10 sick or personal days every year, as well as federal holidays off. In addition, they are entitled to two weeks of paid vacation from you. You should talk to the nanny about this to ensure that he or she takes vacation when you will be able to take care of the children. A good compromise would be the nanny taking vacation during the same time of the year that you do.

- What you expect from the behavior of the nanny should also be addressed in the contract. This includes the use of your phone, inviting individuals over, smoking, and what television programs she should refrain from watching around the children.

- Address the duration of the contract: Is this good for one year at a time?

• Finally, the terms of termination should be completely outlined. In this part of the contract, how much notice each party has to give for termination must be outlined. In addition, reasons as to why you can terminate the employment of the nanny should be outlined so there are no disagreements.

You may hire a lawyer to write the nanny agreement. You want to make sure all your bases are covered so there are no problems between you and your nanny. If you go through an agency or a Web site, each will often have sample forms you can use to create the nanny contract. You can also type one on your computer, outlining everything mentioned here, and simply have the nanny sign it. Ensure that the nanny signs the contract with a witness present, as this is very important for legality. Ensure that you get it notarized. Give the nanny a copy for his or her records.

Finding a nanny who can not only handle your children, but also the household duties, is incredibly important. Although the cost is high, you will be able to concentrate on other things, rather than worry about how you are going to do the laundry and get the kids to soccer practice on time.

ASKING FAMILY AND FRIENDS

Single fathers often ask friends and family to help with child care duties. While this option is usually free, there are often problems with scheduling that can make it hard to find a consistent babysitter for your children.

If you choose to ask your family, you will find more takers than when you ask your friends. Your friends should be able to watch the children on occasion, if you have to go out one night, or are out of town for a few days, but generally they will be busy with their own lives and unable to make the commitment to baby-sit on a daily basis. That does not mean you should not ask them. You may find that one of your friend's spouses enjoys watching children.

Asking family, especially siblings or parents, is a good idea. Generally, your parents will be more than willing to watch the children for free, simply so they can spend time with their grandchildren. If you have gone through a divorce, the children will not see their grandparents as much as they once did, so both your parents and your children will want to take advantage of time together. Your siblings may be able to watch your children, but again it falls into the same problem as with friends. Your siblings have their own families and lives and may not be able to watch your children on a regular basis.

Asking friends and family to take care your children can be a slippery slope to navigate. The best course of action is to tell your family and friends that you are having trouble finding a baby-sitter, but you need to find someone who can watch the children while you are at work because a day care is too expensive. Let them know that you trust them and would rather they watched your children than anyone else. Appealing to them and being honest is the best course of action when asking friends to baby-sit.

Naturally, when you are getting free baby-sitting from friends and family, you may feel like you are being a nuisance. If you find that they are starting to tell you that they cannot always baby-sit (making excuses), or they seem irritated when you ask, consider asking someone else. If you want to show appreciation, but do not have much money, a simple dinner can say thanks. You can either take your friends or family out to eat, or bring them over for dinner. In addition, you can offer to watch their children when they need a baby-sitter. You should always show appreciation to friends and family who help you out. Even if it is doing yard work for your friends and family, you are at least saying thank you.

This is also a good option for your children because they will get to spend time with their grandparents and relatives. Rather than have a sitter they do not know or a nanny they have never met, they can spend time with people they know and trust. More importantly, you will be leaving your children with someone that you trust and you will not have to worry about what may be happening after you leave the house. Your parents, siblings, and friends will take care of your children with the same care and safety as if they were their own children. However, there can be some issues when family members watch your children.

- If your family members baby-sit for free, but you rely on them too much, resentment may build. Remember to always repay the favor.

- Some families make a habit of knowing everyone's business, and if you have a family like that, baby-sitting could create an opportunity to learn more about you. If you prefer privacy, that is something you do not always get when family baby-sits.

- If your children get tired of Grandma and Grandpa and do not want to go anymore, you will have to break the news as gently as possible to your parents. However, they may not take it well.

- It is easy to question how a baby-sitter handles your children, but it may be harder to question how your parents or siblings deal with your children. If they spank and you do not, confronting them about it can lead to a family argument. You can fire a sitter, but you cannot fire your family.

- If you have your parents baby-sit, your siblings may be resentful that they were not asked.

CHAPTER CONCLUSION

Hiring a nanny or baby-sitter can make things easier for you when you are trying to balance work and your children. After you have become a single father, the tasks suddenly required by you can seem overwhelming. You may feel as though you cannot manage without some help, and child care help is something you may need to find.

It is important that you do not rush the process of finding a nanny or sitter. These people will be watching your children and you want to make sure that they are going to do a good job. There have been plenty of stories of parents hiring baby-sitters who seem good on paper, but turn out to be anything but good for their children. This is why the business of nanny cams are so incredibly popular. That being said, most nannies and baby-sitters out there are excellent and ready to help you and your children. They want to work with children and they want to help you manage being a single father. Many single fathers find nannies and sitters who help raise their children through the years, and even become an important part of the child's life.

7 Managing Stress

> "If you ask what is the single most important
> key to longevity, I would have to say it is
> avoiding worry, stress, and tension. And if you
> did not ask me, I'd still have to say it."
>
> — George Burns, American comedian

Stress is all too common in everyone's lives. Even those who are not single fathers suffer from stress, and it can cause serious problems. Stress comes from work, home life, finances, and more. Stress can make it hard to concentrate and, more importantly, it can make it difficult to enjoy life. Simply put, unmanaged stress can be very harmful for your body and mind.

WHAT IS STRESS?

Essentially, stress is the emotional and physical strain put on our bodies and minds, caused by our response to pressure that occurs in the outside world. As a single father, you will find there are a lot of bits of stress that can manifest themselves to yourself.

These include:

- The divorce, if you are going through one, and your battle for custody

- The death of your spouse

- Dealing with your children by yourself

- Balancing the requirements of work, while handling issues at home with your children

- Financial stress can be an issue as you try to juggle your commitments and your own needs

People all know stress when it happens. When you are stressed, you become tense and irritable. Often, you have an inability to concentrate properly and you can sometimes get a headache and fast heartbeat. If you are under stress for a long period of time, it can become serious because it will put a lot of strain on your body.

WHAT CAUSES STRESS?

To better understand stress, it is important to look at what can cause it. If you know what causes your stress, you can combat it better and deal with it accordingly. Each different cause of stress has to be dealt with in a certain way. For a single father, four common causes of stress include your finances, a divorce, your children, and your work.

Finances

In nearly every study done, finances and money have been found to be the leading causes of stress. LifeCare, Inc. (**www.lifecare.**

com), a company that delivers global workplace support services, recently conducted a survey online. They found that 23 percent of the participants named money and finances as the leading causes of stress in their lives. In a study conducted by Readers Digest, people in 16 countries were asked what stressed them out the most, and the majority of respondents said they were very stressed about money. When you are dealing with financial stress, you can experience the following:

- Some financial stress sufferers end up cultivating unhealthy coping behavior. This can include drinking alcohol, smoking, and overeating in an effort to numb the anxiety you are feeling. If you find you are happy when you eat fast food, you will eat more in a never-ending cycle to make yourself happy. The problem is that this behavior only leads to more stress (obesity, sluggish reflexes, and a tendency to never fill the void).

- If you are stressing over your finances, you probably do not have as much money as you would like, which means you do not put enough money into areas of self-care, including the food you eat and the health care you pay for. The problem is that stress can cause illness, and if you stress about finances to the point you do not have any money, you will not be able to pay for the illnesses caused by the stress.

- Many people who suffer anxiety and stress over finances will experience loss of sleep or develop sleepwalking tendencies. This then causes a sleep deficit, which impairs cognitive functions and can create moodiness and irrita-bility. It can also cause problems at work when you have trouble concentrating on the task at hand.

- When you are under financial stress, you can develop unhealthy emotions, including anxiety, frustration, and hopelessness. This adds to the stress you are feeling and it can lead to some serious problems down the road if it is not properly managed.

There are three primary reasons, in regards to your personality, over why you will develop financial problems that can cause you stress. These reasons are:

1. Ignorance: It is not a crime to be ignorant about your finances, but it can cause you a lot of stress. If you do not know how much you have, how much you spend, or how much you earn, you are going to end up getting an unwelcome surprise when the debt starts to pile up.

2. Indulgence: You can be financially secure, but if you like to indulge in the finer things in your life and over spend, you are not going to be doing yourself any favors.

3. Poor planning: Not planning for the death of your spouse or for divorce can result in unwelcome surprises when you suddenly find yourself with half your usual income. Not planning for potential emergencies can leave you financially strapped, as well.

Finances after the death of a spouse

After you lose your spouse, you will get a rude awakening as a part of the income for the house disappears. If you relied on your spouse's income, you will find that there is suddenly little or no money coming into the house. Depending on how much planning you did, you will either have a lot of money or very little. If you had life insurance, you should be financially secure for quite a while. However, if you did not plan for death and hoped for the best, you may need to survive only on social security payments from your spouse's estate. These are usually quite small and will be a big change from what you are used to.

The biggest financial mistakes made during a divorce

The seeds for financial stress following a divorce are created before the divorce is ever completed. On average, a divorce is going to cost you $20,000, which can cause considerable financial stress. Obviously, the faster you make decisions and come to a resolution in the divorce, the more money you are going to save. If you take the time to make good decisions during the divorce, you will be able to protect your finances, at least partly. The main reasons for financial stress during and after a divorce are the following:

1. **Not being aware of your living expenses.** Many people fall into the trap of leaving all the financial decisions to their spouse. When a divorce happens, it can be natural to underestimate your expenses, but that can lead to severe debt. One way to prevent this is to budget and pay attention to what you pay. It is common that when you start thinking about your expenses, you think about your bills and mortgage, but there are many others, including clothing, transportation, entertainment, school costs, insurance, food, and more.

2. **Making assumptions about who gets the house.** There is a common assumption that the custodial parent gets the house, but this is not always the case. Even if it is, you

may not able to afford the mortgage payments anymore, which could result in selling the house and moving somewhere cheaper.

3. **Believing that splitting equally is fair.** When you split everything in a 50/50 manner, you may think that it is fair and that both you and your ex-wife will get enough of an income from the assets. However, this does not always work out in a fair manner. Who gets the expensive car and who gets the cheap car? Who gets the expensive electronics and who gets furniture? Who gets the stock portfolio and who gets the savings account? Often, disagreements over who gets what can cause divorce costs to rise, which can eat into any savings you may have had by going 50/50.

4. **Underestimating alimony and child support.** Probably the biggest mistake you can make is to underestimate how much you may be paying out in support. It can end up costing a lot of money and if you do not plan for it, you will get a big surprise when you suddenly find yourself paying out 25 percent of your income to your ex-wife and kids.

5. **Not thinking about outstanding debt.** When you go through a divorce, the debt is not always equally split. If you have joint credit cards with your ex-wife, you still have to pay those off, even if she racks up a large bill. Credit card companies make both of you responsible for the unsecured debt, so by not paying the credit card she has, she can damage both your credit scores. Even if the judge decreed that your spouse is responsible for paying it off, if it is under both your names, the credit card

company sees it as a shared debt that affects both of your credit scores.

6. **Failure to plan.** The biggest mistake people make in their lives is a failure to plan. If you do not plan for your future, you will get a rude wake up call. Divorce happens in about half of all marriages, so you should plan for the possibility of your marriage ending in divorce. One good way to plan is to get a financial advisor who can look at your new finances and expenses and help you determine how to best plan.

7. **Failure to understand the effect of divorce on finances.** This is part of planning for the future because you need to know how to survive the financial hit of divorce before it happens, not after. If you think your finances will not change after the divorce, you are wrong. Once the divorce is done, there is no going back, and you need to wake up and start planning for your new financial life.

Divorce

If you have gone through a divorce, you will suffer stress — there is no way around it. Divorces are incredibly stressful for both parties, but they can be more so for men. In a 2007 study conducted by Statistics Canada, men between the ages of 20 and 64 were interviewed and researched, and it was found that men were six times more likely to be depressed and stressed when they had gone through a divorce, compared to men who were still married. Women who were recently divorced, however, were only 3.5 times more likely to be stressed and depressed when compared with women who were currently married. In addition, it took men almost four years to get over the stress of the divorce.

Kids

While there is stress, especially when you are juggling the duties of being a single father without any help, there is also the joy of being around your children. There are two ways you will be a single father, through divorce/separation or through becoming a widower. If you are a single father because of divorce, you will have stress relating to custody, but the stress will not come from your kids. You will feel happy to see them every time, and the stress relating to them will be reduced. That does not mean you will not have stress as a divorced father. Depending on the relationship you have with your ex, the children may be fed stories from her to make them resent you. As a result, you could find stress with your kids when they visit because they neither listen to nor respect you.

If you lost your wife through death, you will just be happy to be with your children because they are a link to your lost wife. However, managing the father duties alone can be highly stressful. You not only have to get the kids through the grief of losing their mother, but you have to get through your own grief, manage finances with possibly less income, and juggle all the duties of both a father and mother.

Work

Next to worries about money, work is the biggest cause of stress. In a 2005 LifeCare poll, 21 percent of the respondents said their work was the main cause of their stress. Stress at work can come from many different avenues and can be a significant problem in one's life, especially when you are a single father who is juggling home life and work life. One contributing factor of work stress is that workers are required to work at faster paces to meet the productivity benchmarks set for them by upper management. In a series of studies conducted in the European Union in 1990, 1995, and 2000, the percentage of workers who had to work at higher speeds was increasing. In 1990, 48 percent spent 25 percent of their time working at a fast rate to increase productivity. This increased to 54 percent in 1995 and to 56 percent in 2000. In this same study, 50 percent of workers had tight deadlines roughly 25 percent of the time. By 1995, it increased to 56 percent, and in 2000 it increased to 60 percent. In the United States, according to the Department of Labor, the number of workers working long hours has increased. Roughly 26 percent of men currently work 50 hours or more per week.

Depending on where you are in the company, your stress will differ. When you are low on the company ladder, you will often experience more stress than those who are more powerful in the company.

Some other factors that can influence workplace stress include:

- Pressure to ensure that investors in the company are making money.

- If you are part of a company without a union, you may feel trapped, or that you have no control in your work.

- Rivalries within your workplace can cause stress as you are driven to outperform your co-workers, but in the same amount of time and with the same resources.

- The worry of being laid off from your job if you do not perform up to management's specifications. The problem with this is the more you stress about it, the harder it will be to concentrate on work and, therefore, the more likely you are to be laid off or fired.

- Bullying in the workplace is another problem that can contribute to workplace stress. In a study by Workplace Bullying Institute and Zogby International, 13 percent of U.S. employees were currently bullied, 24 percent said they have been bullied in the past, and 12 percent have seen workplace bullying. Almost half of all workers, 49 percent, have either witnessed or been affected by bullying in the workplace.

Some symptoms of workplace stress include:
- Moodiness and problems with being angry or irritable
- Problems sleeping, just like with financial stress
- Headaches
- Problems with interpersonal relationships
- Upset stomachs
- Psychological distress

SIGNS YOU ARE UNDER STRESS

This book touched on some of the symptoms that can result from being under stress. However, it is important to go into this in more detail so you can see exactly what you should watch for to deal with stress properly.

If you are under stress, you could experience some of the following:
- Muscle tension in your shoulders, back, neck, chest, and limbs

- An increase in blood pressure
- Lack of motivation
- No energy
- Aggravation of preexisting conditions, such as asthma or allergies
- Getting ill more often
- No interest in sex, or experiencing sexual dysfunction
- Nightmares
- Problems sleeping or developing sleepwalking
- You may find you are extra jumpy or reactive
- You cannot concentrate and you feel distracted
- You worry a great deal about things that should not be a big concern
- You miss deadlines
- You feel disorientated
- Heartbeat increases
- Breathing increases
- Sweating
- Increasing headaches
- No appetite
- Overeating
- Trouble digesting food
- Diarrhea or constipation
- You begin to use drugs or alcohol to manage the stress you are feeling

WHAT HEALTH PROBLEMS DOES STRESS CAUSE?

If you deal with stress on a daily basis, you can develop chronic stress, which is very dangerous. When you are stressed, the fight–or–flight response is often initiated, which comes from our evolutionary past to help us escape from dangerous situations, like being hunted by a wild animal. When stress occurs, your adrenalin increases, your heart rate shoots up, your digestion slows, blood flows more to muscles, and nervous functions change. All this is done to give us a burst of energy and strength. These days, our flight-or-fight response is being activated in areas where it has absolutely no use, and it is being activated constantly, which puts an incredible amount of strain on the body. As a result, our physical well-being suffers. In fact, some estimates show that 90 percent of all cases doctors see are a result of stress.

When you first start dealing with chronic stress, you may find that you get sick more often and have an increased susceptibility to colds and headaches. As your exposure to chronic stress increases, the ill effects on your body can get much worse. Some problems your body can develop because of stress include:

- Depression
- Hair loss
- Heart disease
- Hyperthyroidism
- Obesity
- Diabetes
- Obsessive Compulsive Disorder
- Anxiety disorder

- Tooth and gum disease
- Ulcers or Irritable Bowel Syndrome
- Cancer
- Erectile dysfunction

Relating to the most serious of these conditions, the National Cancer Institute has conducted studies over the past 30 years that link stress to cancer. There have been various links found between stress and an increased risk of cancer, but no direct link (cause and effect) has been found between cancer and chronic stress. Various studies have found that chronic stress weakens the immune system, which allows virus-related tumors to flood the body. Recent studies have found that the neuroendocrine response of humans, which is when more hormones go into the blood to stimulate the nervous system during times of stress, causes an alteration in the processes of cells that help fight cancer, as well as repair DNA and regulate cell growth.

MANAGING STRESS

Naturally, you will want to deal with stress to stop it from not only shortening your life, but making the time you do have on Earth less enjoyable. There are many different ways to manage stress, and several of them will be covered here.

Spending time with the kids

You have a few great stress reducers right in front of you, and they are called your children. No doubt, your children can be sources of stress, but they can also be a great way to relieve stress. When you have a bad day at work or worry about money and come home to find your children smiling at you, it makes everything better.

Spending time with your children, playing with them, and talking with them can help you feel more grounded and your stress will begin to melt away.

Get a hobby

You need to find something to get your mind off of being stressed. This can be something that makes you feel better and simultaneously acts as a stress-reducer. Having a hobby is a great way to reduce the amount of stress you feel.

There are a wide variety of hobbies that you can get involved in, but it is important that you choose a hobby that is not going to cause you more stress. For example, building a ship in a glass bottle is a great hobby, but if you are getting stressed while doing it, the hobby will only cause problems. Your hobby needs to be relaxing. Some great hobbies you can look at include:

- Gardening: This can be relaxing and rewarding. When you spend the day out in your garden and see the fruits of your labors (quite literally), you may feel content.

- Fishing: If you are sitting in a boat on a nice, quiet day and are casting off your fishing rod into the water, you will feel relaxed and peaceful. Few things can stress you on a nice summer morning while fishing in a lake that is in the middle of nowhere.

- Collecting: It is surprising how much collecting can help you with stress. When you finally get that baseball card you were looking for or manage to get a rare stamp, you will feel rewarded. If your work brings you stress, buying collectibles with the money you make can help make that stress worthwhile, and help you reduce it at work. Just keep reminding yourself why you are working and you will not feel as stressed.

- Knitting/needlepoint: Yes, you are a man, but that does not mean you cannot do needlepoint or knitting. In fact, there are many men who knit and needlepoint as a way of relaxing. Some prominent men have practiced knitting, including Russell Crowe. If he can knit, so can you. You may also need the skill when your kids' clothes tear or when something else in the house needs mending.

- Models: Model trains are surprisingly adept at making people relax. Much like with collecting, you are focusing on something other than your stress. You can make vast landscapes with model trains, find others who share the enthusiasm, and develop a love of something you may have never thought you would enjoy. In addition, if you like to make models, you will find this is a great hobby that helps you relax as you focus on putting together the little pieces of a model for a desired end result.

- Courses at a local community college: This can help you find friends, do something you love, and keep you busy all at once. Visit your community college's Web site to review the course schedule. Public libraries also sometimes hold free courses, such as Spanish conversation classes and needlepoint lessons.

- Recreational sports: Few things are better than spending time with your friends. One of the best ways to have fun with your friends is to go out and get involved in recreational sports. Whether it is baseball, football, running, or just having a game of three-on-three basketball, you will find that playing sports helps burn energy, it makes you happier, and it helps alleviate the stress that you are feeling in your life.

- Home renovations: Most building supply stores offer classes to show you how to complete simple renovating projects, such as laying down tile, painting your house, or building a new wall.

- Automotive: Working on a car is relaxing and allows you to focus on something other than your stress. When you are working on a car, you are solving problems, which can be a good way for your brain to get away from stress. If you have not worked on a car before, you can join an automotive class at a local community college and learn everything you need to know. This not only gets you out of the house and away from a source of stress, but it also helps you meet new friends.

- Video games: Sometimes when you are feeling down, nothing is a better pick me up than solving puzzles, shooting aliens, or competing with your favorite athletes. Video games have been shown to help alleviate stress in many studies, so if you just want to stay home for a weekend, this can be a great way to take it easy.

Music

Several studies show that music, specifically classical music, reduces stress — whether you are playing it or listening to it. One study published in the Medical Science Monitor in 2005 found that playing a musical instrument reversed multiple components of human stress. As with hobbies, you are focusing your mind on something else when you attempt to play a musical instrument.

However, listening to music can also help. The Cochrane Systematic Review found that listening to music lowers blood pressure, heart rates, and anxiety levels of those people who suffer from heart problems, many of which are created from stress.

Exercising

One of the best things you can do for yourself if you are stressed is exercise. Exercising not only helps your mental well-being, but it can help you get in shape, make you healthier, and help you live longer. Many studies have been conducted that show the positive impact exercising has on stress. In one study conducted by the National Intramural- Recreational Sports Association, the two biggest benefits from exercise were improved emotions and reduced stress. The reason for this is as follows:

1.   Exercise improves blood flow to your brain, which brings more oxygen and sugars that are needed for the brain to work properly and at peak capacity.

2.   Exercise releases endorphins into the blood stream, which make you feel happy and provide a positive effect on your overall mood and mental well-being.

3.   Exercise relaxes tense muscles, which can help lower stress levels.

4.   Exercise helps you sleep better. The better you sleep, the more rested you will be, and the better able you will be to combat stress in your day-to-day life.

Stress is sometimes described as a build-up of inactivity and over-thinking without any possibility of release. Exercise gives a physical release that diminishes the frustration that one feels in his or her mind.

Yoga

Yoga originated in India thousands of years ago as an important part of meditation, another great stress reliever. While well-known in Asia for thousands of years, it has only been in the last few decades that yoga has become popular in the Western world and has become something that individuals do regularly to help manage their stress. Medical studies in the past few decades have found that yoga has several beneficial effects on the body, including:

- Reduced stress
- Improved sleep
- Reduced cortisol levels (referred to as the "stress hormone")
- Relief from allergies and asthma
- Lowered blood pressure
- Lowered heart rate
- Reduced anxiety
- Reduced muscle tension
- Increased strength
- Increased flexibility

The style most cited as the best for dealing with stress is the hatha yoga style. This type of yoga helps to create a calmer mind while improving flexibility, which in turn reduces tension in the muscles, helps you sleep, and reduces headaches due to better blood flow to the brain. YogaFinder.com is a great resource to help you find a yoga class in your area. It also includes where to find yoga teacher training courses, yoga events, yoga music artists, yoga products, and a directory of retreat centers. Visit **www.yogafinder.com** for these resources. Findyoga.com can also direct you to classes to try.

Before joining a yoga class, consider these things:

- The instructor should have proper qualifications for yoga. Find out where he or she learned yoga and how long he or she has been teaching yoga.

- Do you have any physical problems that may require special attention, including bad knees or a chronic sore back? Your yoga instructor should be able to give you tips and hints.

- Are you able to get into a class that is meant for beginners, and can you follow along in your first class?

- What is the focus of the class? You want one focused on relaxation and stress management.

- Find out what you need for the class, including a yoga mat and clothing

Meditation

When you are stressed, it is very important to find a way to relax and calm yourself. There are few better ways to do this than with meditation. As mentioned before, when the body is stressed, it is operating on the principle of "fight or flight." Prolonged stress becomes chronic stress and can cause serious problems for the body. Meditation is different; it acts in the opposite manner. Instead of stressing the body and making it agitated, it returns the body to a calm state, allowing the body to fix the problems and prevents new problems and damage from occurring.

Prayer is also a common form of meditation that many people find relaxing and comforting. It can reduce stress and make people feel happier as they become more in tune with their spirituality.

This has been found by several studies. In a recent study conducted by Chinese researchers and scientists at the University of Oregon, the effects of meditation on stress were found to be quite amazing. Their findings were published in the *Proceedings of the National Academy of Sciences* journal. The study consisted of 80 students in two groups of 40. One group received five days of meditation training that consisted of not trying to control thought and relying on a restful state of alertness, increasing the body-mind awareness while getting breathing guidance from an instructor as soothing music played. The other group received basic relaxation training. Each group was tested before and after for their reactions to mental stress and their ability to pay attention. Before the training, the groups were similar in both their alertness and attention span. However, after the training, the group that meditated for five days had lower levels of anxiety, anger, fatigue, and depression. They also released less cortisol, which allowed them to control their stress better.

To help you meditate, follow these instructions to the best of your ability:

1.   Make time to meditate each day. Meditation as part of your daily routine will work much better, just like exercising. If you exercise once per week, you will not get the same results as if you exercise once per day. When you choose to meditate, take the following into consideration:

   a. Typically, five minutes is a good length of time for meditation, but you can go longer if you want.

b. You can meditate at any point during the day, but the morning is often better because you have not gone through a day of stress and will not be tired from the events of the day.

c. You should not meditate right after you eat or if you are hungry.

2. Look for a quiet place to meditate. It should be free of any noise, television, phones, or appliances that make noise. You can have gentle music playing, but only as long as it is calm, soothing, and does not affect your concentration.

3. Sit down on level ground with a cushion under you if you find the ground uncomfortable. Unlike the typical look of a meditating individual with their legs crossed in an uncomfortable way, you do not have to assume any unusual positions. Just ensure that your back is straight. You can sit in a chair to make sure your back is straight. As long as you are in a relaxed position, with your back straight, you can meditate. You can try meditating while lying down, but you may end up falling asleep.

4. When you meditate, keep your eyes half-open. You can choose to not focus on anything, or you can focus on something steady, like the flame on a candle.

5. Begin to take deep breaths that begin in your abdomen. Feel your stomach rising and falling. Your breathing should be done in the following manner:

a. Breathe in and hold for a count of three.

b. Breathe out for a count of three.

    c.   Repeat for 15 to 20 minutes.

6.   Begin to relax every muscle in your body. This does not mean to suddenly relax your body. Start with your toes and slowly work up to your head, allowing the tension and stress to melt away as your body relaxes.

7.   Find an anchor for your mind, which is where you focus your attention. You want to focus on something so that the noise in your head will fade away as you focus only on one thing.

8.   You can recite a mantra-like "om" over and over in a steady rhythm, but it is not required. Often, it is simply better to count each breath as it happens.

9.   Think of a place that keeps you calm and helps you relax.

10.   You will need to silence your mind. This is done by focusing on one thing and then beginning to focus on nothing at all. This will not happen quickly and it often takes a great deal of meditation to get it right and to be able to do it.

When you meditate, take into consideration your mood when you are not meditating. After you meditate, you will feel calm and happier. On the days you do not meditate, you will notice you are more stressed and irritable. One thing you may worry about with meditating is losing track of time. If you think about time as you meditate, you will have trouble concentrating and focusing. Use a gentle timer that emits a soft sound to alert you that your time is up. You do not want an alarm that starts making a lot of noise because the anticipation of this can distract you.

You can also use the principles of meditation elsewhere to deal with stress. For example, if you are getting stressed, take a few moments to visualize a place that makes you happy and practice relaxed breathing, as you do when you meditate.

Positive thinking

Another thing you can do is to focus your mind on something other than what is causing you stress. According to the Mayo Clinic (**www.mayoclinic.com**), positive thinking and optimism has a large effect on health. Some of the health benefits of positive thinking that researchers have found include:

- Longer life span
- Decreased depression
- Decreased levels of distress
- Greater resistance to the common cold
- Better mental well-being
- Reduced risk for cardiovascular disease
- Better coping in times of stress

It is important to know when you are experiencing negative thinking and when you are experiencing positive thinking. If you usually think negatively, you need to make a deliberate, focused effort to start maintaining positive thoughts.

Negative thinking often comes in the following forms:

1. You will often focus on only the negative aspects of something instead of on the positive. For example, if you are playing baseball and you hit a double, make several great plays, and score a run, but strike out twice, you will focus

on striking out rather than the great way you played for the rest of the game.

2.   You will blame yourself when something bad occurs. For example, if a client cancels a business meeting, you assume he cancels because you are not good at your job.

3.   If you constantly anticipate the worst, you are guilty of negative thinking. If you do not change your routine because you think something bad will happen, or you do not make friends because you assume people will not like you, you are on a destructive negative thinking path.

4.   You may see things as only good or bad, or black and white, and this is a very polarizing negative view. In this regard, you feel you have to be perfect, otherwise you are a complete failure. An example of this is hitting 50 home runs a season every year, but never hitting 60 home runs. You may see yourself as a failure as a result.

If you are guilty of these negative-thinking forms, you are only adding stress to your life and need to find a way to be positive. Positive thinking is good for you and can change your entire outlook on life. It takes practice and time, but you can develop a positive thinking habit if you are committed to it. Here are some ways that you can think positively.

1.   Every so often during the day, stop what you are doing and evaluate what you are thinking about. If you are thinking negatively, take those thoughts and put a positive spin on them. If you are thinking that you have to get your car repaired and will need to take the bus for the next two weeks, look at it this way: You get to sit on a bus,

read a book, and not worry about trying to get somewhere during a commute.

2. You should be ready to laugh and smile at yourself during trying times. Look for humor anywhere you can — laughter is a great stress reliever.

3. Exercise, as previously mentioned, reduces stress and can make you happier. Exercise three times per week to improve your mood and reduce your overall stress. Also, eat healthy so your body has the fuel it needs to deal with stress.

4. If you are around negative people most of the time, try to surround yourself with positive people. You want to have supportive people in your life, and anyone who only takes is not someone you want around.

5. Most importantly, you should practice positive self-talk. One way you can do this is to not say anything about yourself that you would not say to another person. Be kind to yourself.

Positive thinking works. In a study by researchers at the University of Wisconsin, regions of the brain that are activated when negative thoughts appear will weaken the immune response to the flu vaccine in people. The reason for this is that more electrical activity in the brain's prefrontal cortex creates a weaker immune system as much as six months later. The right prefrontal cortex is active during anger, fear, and sadness, while the left prefrontal cortex is active with feelings of being upbeat and happy. In the study, greater activity in this portion of the brain led to a stronger immune response against the flu.

This is the reason positive thinking can go a very long way in helping lower stress. When you think in an upbeat manner, you help your body and mind. You are making it easier for your body to fight diseases and respond to stress. When you think negatively, you are not only creating stress in situations where it should not exist (worrying about something happening that has not happened yet), but you are hurting your body and mind, as well.

A simple smile can go a long way; if you make the effort to smile, you will find that your overall outlook during the day improves. It also gets other people smiling and helps those people be happier, too.

CHAPTER CONCLUSION

Being a single father is not easy. It involves a lot of work and effort and that can manifest itself in stress. Stress is something you do not want to have. It leads to serious problems over prolonged periods and can result in illness or death. You have to find ways to manage the stress in your life. You may not be able to get rid of the things that are causing you stress, but you can look for ways to work around those things to minimize your stress.

Meditation, yoga, positive thinking, and setting aside personal time for yourself are all important options to consider for stress relief. You need to be able take the stress and find an outlet for it. Be creative: start with a hobby, or simply find time to relax with yoga and meditation.

No matter how you choose to deal with stress, it must be dealt with. Ignoring the stress or hoping it goes away is like trying to stop a flood by turning your back to it. You may forget about it for a little while, but eventually it is going to sweep you away.

"The most interesting information comes from children, for they tell all they know and then stop."

— Mark Twain

3

The Roles of the Father

"Fathers, like mothers, are not born. Men grow into fathers and fathering is a very important stage in their development."
— David Gottesman, American businessman

8 Doctor

> *"The fact is that child rearing is a long, hard job, the rewards are not always immediately obvious, the work is undervalued, and parents are just as human and almost as vulnerable as their children."*
>
> — Benjamin Spock, Dr. Spock's Baby and Child Care

As a single father, you need to assume a variety of roles. In this section, we will go over all of them, but this chapter addresses being a doctor. You need to ensure that your children are well and healthy. The healthier they are, the happier they will be and the longer they will live. By knowing how to help your children when they are sick and helping to keep them healthy, you can save yourself a lot of worry and stress.

HEALTH ISSUES TO WATCH FOR

As a father, especially a single father, you may worry about your children too much. If you lost your wife to disease or illness, that worry can be overwhelming as you fixate on ensuring that your children do not pass away like your wife did. The truth is that your children will get sick. There is no way to avoid it. They go to school with hundreds of children, so they will inevitably get sick. However, just because they get sick, that does not mean they are going to die.

Below is a list of the most common childhood illnesses and symptoms to watch for, as well as what you need to do if your child becomes sick with one of these illnesses.

Chicken pox

Everyone knows about chicken pox and most have had it. It can still be a cause for concern when it appears, though, if a parent does not immediately recognize it for what it is. Chicken pox comes in the form of an itchy rash with red spots all over the body. It is caused by a virus that spreads easily and can pass between people through sneezing, coughing, physical touch, and more. Typically, a person who has chicken pox can spread the virus before he or she shows symptoms, usually within the first two or three days before the rash appears.

The first symptoms of chicken pox are:

- Fever
- Headache
- Sore throat
- Tiredness
- Lack of appetite

The rash will appear one to two days after the first symptoms start. After the rash appears, it takes about seven days to get through the illness, with new red spots appearing every day for up to a week. Thankfully, the treatment for chicken pox is simply to rest and take medicine to treat any fevers. To help with the itching, soak your children in an oatmeal bath.

Colic

If your children are still babies, one thing you may have to deal with is colic. Colic is a condition that some babies develop, which causes a healthy baby to cry and scream frequently and for extended periods of time with no discernible cause. Colic is not dangerous for the baby, but it can be horrible for you. You will have to listen to your baby crying constantly for weeks on end, with little you can do to help him or her. Babies cry often, so sometimes you may not know if your baby is crying because he or she is cranky or because he or she has colic. Generally, babies will not cry for hours at a time, so doctors use the "three-pattern" to diagnose colic. If your baby cries for more than three consecutive hours a day, for at least three days a week, for at least three weeks in a row, it may be colic. Between the age of 6 and 8 weeks, colic will generally be the worst; from 8 to 14 weeks, it will disappear and never return.

It is not known what causes colic, but doctors theorize that it may be caused by temperament and an immature nervous system. It is important to remember with colic that:

1.   It is not caused by pain or illness

2.   It is not your fault

3.   It is not your baby's fault

To help with colic and make it less severe, you can do the following:

1.   Rock the baby in a quiet room

2.   Take him or her out for a walk in a stroller

3.   Take the baby for a ride in the car

4.   Let him or her listen to a white-noise sound, like a fan

5.   Comfort your baby as best you can

6.   Have the baby lay on his or her stomach along your forearm, with his or her head resting in your hand

Croup

Croup is common in young children and usually occurs in the fall and winter months. It is easily recognizable by the harsh and bark-ing cough your child may experience. The voice box may swell and narrow, as will the windpipe and breathing tubes to the lungs. As a result, it can be difficult for your child to breathe when he or she has croup. The important thing to remember is that croup is not serious and will generally pass with a few days of rest at home.

Croup is caused by the same viruses that cause the common cold, and it is very contagious. Hand washing is important to prevent the spread of croup. Typical symptoms of croup include:

- Barking cough

- Raspy voice

- Harsh noise when breathing in

- Elevated breathing

Symptoms get worse at night, and your child may wake up several times in the middle of the night for two to three days. Croup should pass within five days. It is not necessary to take your child to the doctor if he or she suffers from croup, as home care can cure it.

If your child is having a croup attack, do the following:

1. Sooth your child and reassure him or her because crying can cause swelling of the windpipe and make it harder for him or her to breathe.

2. Turn on hot water in the shower so the air can fill with steam. Sit with your child in the bathroom for at least 10 minutes — moist air helps breathing during a croup attack. You can also have your child sit over a humidifier, or carefully lean over a pot of boiling water.

3. Cold air helps, so dress your child in warm clothes and take him or her outside into the cool, fresh air for about 10 minutes.

4. Ensure that your child is well-hydrated and has popsicles and ice drinks several times an hour.

If you do these things during a croup attack and your child does not get better within a week, or continues having an attack for 30 minutes or more, take him or her to the doctor. If you are extremely worried, take him or her to the emergency room.

Ear infection

Ear infections can be common in children, and they are caused when germs from the nose and throat get trapped in the middle ear behind the eardrum. When your child has a cold, the tube that connects the ear to the throat can swell and become blocked, which then traps fluid in the ear. Children get ear infections more frequently because they have small tubes that can become blocked more easily. The symptom of an ear infection is an ear ache that can be painful at times. A fever can also develop, and there may be yellow fluid coming from the ears.

An ear infection will usually go away on its own, but you can get some over-the-counter children's pain reliever if you want to dull the pain for your child. Because ear infections can be dangerous, going to your doctor may be advisable if you worry. You can also get prescription ear drops that will help deal with the pain.

Fifth disease

You may have never heard of it, but fifth disease is a very common childhood illness. Some people call it "slapped cheek disease" because it creates a rash on the face of children. The disease can be spread through coughing and sneezing, and can be quite contagious. The disease is caused by a virus, and symptoms include:

- Runny nose
- Sore throat
- Headache
- Rash

The rash will be all over the rest of the body and takes two to five days to fade away. It is easily treated with rest and fluids. The disease will disappear within two to three weeks. Once your child's rash appears, he or she can no longer spread the disease to anyone else. However, the rash may come back if your child is under stress or is too warm.

German measles or Rubella

Caused by the Rubella virus, German measles is a mild illness that does not cause any long-term problems in children. It is passed through fluids in the mucous membranes of the nose, and can be spread through sneezing, coughing, sharing food, and talking. If your child touches a surface with droplets of contaminated fluid and then touches his or her eyes, nose, or mouth, he or she can get the virus.

Symptoms of Rubella include:

- Mild fever
- Swollen glands behind the ear

- Skin rash that covers the face, neck, and chest
- Fever
- Eye pain
- Sore throat
- Body aches

A child with Rubella will be contagious for five to seven days, or until the rash appears. However, your child can have the virus dormant in him or her for two or three weeks before symptoms begin to appear. Treatment for Rubella usually consists of children's acetaminophen.

Mumps

Mumps is a very common childhood disease that causes painful swelling of the salivary glands, located between the ear and the jaw. Swelling is not always seen, as one-third of people with mumps will not experience any swelling at all. The illness is spread if someone infected with it sneezes near your child, coughs near him or her, or shares food or drinks with your child.

The symptoms of mumps include:

- Abdominal pain
- Swollen cheeks
- Swollen/painful testicles
- Flu-like symptoms

Roughly 20 percent of all individuals who get the mumps virus will not show any symptoms. When someone becomes infected with the mumps virus, he or she will carry it for several weeks before becoming contagious. They are contagious one to two days before the symptoms start, and will remain contagious for five to nine days after the symptoms first appear. The treatment for mumps involves rest and care at home. Only in extreme cases is there a need for hospitalization. If you take your child into the doctor, he or she may prescribe medicines like acetaminophen to relieve discomfort and reduce the fever.

Pink eye

The dreaded pink eye is something that is very noticeable and highly contagious. It appears as redness and swelling on the eye surface and eye lids. This also causes the eye to emit mucus. Although it looks bad, it is not serious and will disappear within a week or so without any need for medical treatment. However, for children over the age of three, doctors may prescribe Patanol, which can relieve pink eye with two drops per day.

Typical symptoms of pink eye include:

- Redness of the eye
- Swollen and red eyelids
- Tearing
- Itching
- Burning

- Sensitivity to light

- Drainage from the eye in the form of mucus

Typically, pink eye is caused by the infection of bacteria or viruses. It can also be caused by dry eyes due to exposure to wind and sun, chemicals, and allergies. Pink eye is highly contagious and can easily spread. If your child develops pink eye, keep him or her out of school or day care until the symptoms improve. Do not let your child touch his or her eyes; if he or she does, make sure your child thoroughly washes his or her hands.

Roseola

Caused by a virus, roseola is a mild illness that is common in children between the ages of six months and two years. It is extremely rare for a child older than four to get it. The virus is spread by droplets of fluid from the nose and throat, and can be spread by laughing, talking, sneezing, and coughing. If your child develops roseola, you should keep him or her at home until one day after he or she has shown no fever symptoms.

Symptoms of roseola include:

- Sudden fever that rises to between 103 to 105 degrees Fahrenheit and stays for two to three days

- Rash that appears on the torso, neck, and arms after the fever has appeared, and will last one to two days

- Sore throat (rare)

- Stomach ache (rare)

- Vomiting (rare)

- Diarrhea (rare)

Typically, the rash will go away without any medical treatment at all. However, use of acetaminophen and sponge baths can help treat your child. While the virus looks bad, it is generally harmless for children. However, if your child displays any of the following conditions, contact your doctor:

1. The rash gets worse over several days, instead of disappearing

2. The fever does not disappear after three days

3. A new rash develops and stays around for more than one week

4. The symptoms in your child have become worse and more frequent as the days and weeks go on

Tonsillitis

When there is an infection or inflammation of the tonsils, it is often called tonsillitis. Typically, tonsillitis will last four to ten days. It is caused by a virus, and is spread through the air in droplets when a person breathes, coughs, or sneezes. Symptoms for tonsillitis include:

- Sore throat

- Swollen tonsils
- Swollen throat
- Fever
- Runny nose
- Sneezing
- Coughing

Typically, tonsillitis will go away on its own through home care. You can ease the pain your child feels by having him or her gargle warm salt water, or by making warm tea for him or her. If you worry that your child may have strep throat, you should take him or her to the doctor for antibiotics. An indicator of strep throat is the appearance of white spots in the back of the throat. The doctor will usually not recommend the removal of the tonsils, except in severe cases where the tonsils have become inflamed.

Urinary tract infection

An infection of the urinary tract is caused when germs or bacteria get into the urinary tract, causing infection there and possibly the bladder and kidneys.

In babies and young children, watch for these symptoms:

- Fever
- Dark urine that has a noticeably odd or strange smell
- Loss of appetite
- Vomiting

- Fussiness

Children who are two or older will have the following symptoms:

- Pain and burning when they urinate
- Urinating more often than normal
- Inability to control the bladder
- Urine that smells bad
- Urine that is red, pink, very dark, or cloudy
- Pain in the lower back

For a urinary tract infection, your child will need to take medication for one to two weeks. It is important to ensure that your child takes all of the doctor-prescribed medication over the prescribed time. Do not stop if your child feels better, as the infection can come back. Also, make sure your child drinks plenty of fluids (especially cranberry juice) so he or she can flush out the germs. Remind your child to go to the bathroom each time he or she drinks to empty out the bladder.

Whooping cough

One of the more severe illnesses your child can develop is whooping cough. Highly contagious, whooping cough spreads quickly can cause severe coughing that may last for months. In some cases, your child may cough so much and so hard that he or she ends up hurting a rib.

Whooping cough is very serious for young children and can develop into pneumonia. Typically, most children will recover with little or no problems. Unlike chicken pox, measles, and the mumps, whooping cough can be caught several times, years apart. The illness is caused by a bacteria that infects the top of the throat, which then bothers the throat and causes the coughing. The coughing allows the disease to spread from person to person. Once infected, symptoms appear in a person within seven to 14 days. When your child gets whooping cough, he or she will go through three different stages of the disease:

- **Stage One:** The symptoms in this stage are much like those of a cold. Your child will have a mild cough, runny nose, and watery eyes. There may also be a mild fever. Typically, these symptoms will last a few days to roughly two weeks. The disease is most likely to spread during this time.

- **Stage Two:** While the symptoms of the cold appear to get better, the coughing gets worse. The coughing will become a severe cough that cannot be controlled in your child. Sometimes he or she can cough so hard for so long that he or she may have trouble breathing. After he or she coughs, your child may throw up, and will be very tired. When the child is between his or her coughing fits, he or she will feel perfectly normal. Typically, this stage will last between two and four weeks.

- **Stage Three:** In this stage, your child will feel better, but the cough will get louder. The coughing fits will be less frequent and will usually flare up if your child gets sick with the cold. Typically, this stage can last more than four weeks. Antibiotics are often used to treat whooping cough. Taking antibiotics in the first stage will keep the cough from lasting very long. If your children are very young, they should be taken to the doctor. You can also buy cough syrups, but these typically do not work with whooping cough. Having a humidifier in your child's room and ensuring he or she has enough fluids is important.

Antibiotics are often used to treat whooping cough. Taking antibiotics in the first stage will keep whooping cough from lasting for very long. If your children are very young, then they should be taken to the doctor. You can also buy cough syrups, but these typically do not work with whooping cough. Having a humidifier in your child's room and ensuring he has enough fluids is very important.

TEACHING YOUR CHILDREN ABOUT GERMS

It is very important to teach your children about germs and what germs can do. The more your children know about germs, the better they will be at avoiding them and the healthier they will be.

First, you should read your children books that show them how to practice good hygiene. Four books that are often used include:

- *Germs Make Me Sick* by Melvin Berger

- *Oh, The Things You Can Do That Are Good For You* by Tish Rabe

- *Germs Are Not For Sharing* by Elizabeth Verdick

- *Wash Your Hands* by Tony Ross

You can visually show your children how germs are spread, which will help them learn better. Explaining that germs are microbes they cannot see may help them know what germs are, but they will have trouble relating to them as a threat and may not heed your warnings. One good tip is to cover your child's hands in flour and say that it represents germs. Have your child touch things around the house, such as the bathroom door or living room wall. This shows him or her how germs can spread and stay on surfaces. Count all the places where there is flour to show the amount of germs that can spread through simple actions.

Once you have found all the areas where there are germs, have your child clean up his or her hands to get rid of all the oil. Have him or her use soap and warm water, then show your child how to towel off. Once he or she is done, have him or her touch various things in the house to show how nothing is left over anymore.

It is also important to teach how to properly sneeze and cough. Instead of coughing into hands, as has been the case for decades, teach your child to sneeze and cough into his or her sleeve or the crook of his or her arm.

Your children look up to you as their father, so lead by example. Wash your hands throughout the day, including:

- When you use the bathroom

- Before you handle food

- After you handle food

- After you go to the park

- After going to the grocery store

- At school

- At the library

You should also carry wipes so you can use to wash your and your childrens' hands quickly.

EQUIPMENT YOU NEED ON HAND

Just like a doctor who has to carry his equipment with him, you need to act as Dr. Dad and have all the equipment to help your children when they have bumps, bruises, cuts, and scrapes.

- Make sure you have a first aid book in the home. The American Red Cross issues the *American Red Cross First Aid and Safety Handbook,* which is generally considered to be the go-to manual for first aid in the United States. Generally, it costs about $15 and can be ordered through Amazon.com. You can also look at a copy of it on the American Red Cross' publications Web site at **www. redcross.org/pubs**. Having this manual will help you deal with the minor injury issues that pop up in your home.

- Thermometers are important, so you should have an oral thermometer in your home. Oral thermometers are quite accurate. You can also get a rectal thermometer, which are the most accurate.

- Tweezers are surprisingly useful for first aid. Your child will get hurt and may need pieces of wood, metal bits, or even insects removed, and tweezers can do that. If you need to remove an insect, it is usually a tick. Ticks can cause Lyme disease, which can be serious. When you remove the tick, pull it straight out; do not twist it, as you could leave the head behind.

- Children like to play outdoors, which can lead to hives, itches, rashes, and bee stings. It will be handy to have antihistamines available to deal with these issues. If you live in an area with poison ivy, calamine lotion would be good to have. It alleviates irritation caused by the rash created by the plant.

- Although children like to play outside, they may not fully understand the dangers of skin cancer. Have sunscreen on hand so you can keep your children from getting sunburned. Apply liberally on sunny and cloudy days.

- Bandages are an absolute must when you have children. They are going to get cuts and scrapes, and a bandage will help the wound heal quicker. It is a good idea to get a bandage that has a favorite cartoon character on it.

- Antibiotic ointment is handy when your child has a cut that needs to be disinfected. Before you use antibiotic ointment, wash the wound with water and soap and let it dry.

- Sometimes your child will be in pain, and you will want to help. You may not know what you can give your child to help him or her deal with the pain, but children's acetaminophen is usually a good bet. Do not use aspirin, as it can cause a neurological disorder called Reye's syndrome in children. Talk with your pediatrician about pain relievers to safely give your child.

WHEN SHOULD YOU GO TO THE DOCTOR?

Many parents, even single fathers, will want to take their children to the doctor the minute symptoms appear. It is hard not to rush your children to the pediatrician if you think something is wrong, but your children usually only need tender love and care from you and rest on the couch. Of course, knowing when to take your children to the doctor is important, but it will depend on the symptoms that your children are experiencing.

Fever

There are many childhood illnesses that can cause a fever. Many of these illnesses only need bed rest and fluids to beat. Depending on the age of your child, you will respond differently.

- Under three months old: Take your child to the pediatrician if he or she has a fever above 100 degrees Fahrenheit

- Between three and six months old: Take your child to the pediatrician if he or she has a fever above 101 degrees Fahrenheit

- Above the age of six months: Take your child to the pediatrician if he or she has a fever above 103 degrees Fahrenheit

Watch your child if he or she has a fever. If he or she is playing and alert and has no trouble eating, you should not worry.

Vomiting

Vomiting can look very serious, and it can be hard for you as a father not to rush your child to the doctor when you hear him or her throwing up. If your child vomits three times or less, it is generally not cause for concern. However, there are cases where you do need to take your child to the doctor.

1. If he or she is getting dehydrated, urinating less, or getting a dry mouth.

2. If your child's vomit is dark green. This is a sign of an intestinal obstruction.

3. If your child is a less than one year, or is a newborn.

4. If your child has a severe headache.

5. If your child has abdominal pain, which can be a sign of appendicitis.

Coughing

Coughing can be common in children with colds, so you do not need to send your child to the doctor if he or she has a small cough. However, if your child shows cold symptoms for longer than three to five days, or is not improving after two weeks, take him or her to the doctor. Also, if your child complains about ear pain or difficulty breathing, take him or her to the doctor for a check-up.

Difficulty breathing

When your child has a cold, he or she can develop a wheeze because of a viral upper respiratory tract infection. If he or she is having trouble breathing, call the doctor. This is especially true if your child begins to breathe harder and faster, or if you can see his or her ribs moving in and out.

Dehydration

If your child has diarrhea or is vomiting on a regular basis, he or she will become dehydrated. Signs of dehydration include:

- Urinating less frequently
- Dry mouth
- No tears when crying
- Sunken eyes
- Not as active
- Irritable

Generally, you do not have to take your child to the doctor when he or she is dehydrated; just need to make sure he or she starts drinking water to rehydrate. Dehydration is typically caused by diarrhea because of the large amount of fluid lost. Changing a child's diet to something healthier is a good way to keep away dehydration.

If your child is older than two, give him or her a sports drink to replenish electrolytes.

Lethargic

If your child is lethargic, it could be a cause for concern. Common causes of lethargy are depression and stress. However, it can also be caused by meningitis or a viral infection. Lethargy usually means your child is unable to, or has difficulty, waking up. This does not mean your child is tired or does not have energy; it means he or she can barely move. In that case, take him or her to the doctor. If your child usually runs around the house playing, and one day lays around watching television, that does not mean he or she is lethargic.

Rashes

Rashes can come from many different places and illnesses, including poison ivy, chicken pox, fifth disease, and roseola. If your child develops a rash and a fever at the same time, or if the rash is purple, take him or her to the doctor. Also, if you touch the rash and the color does not fade when you press the rash, take your child to the doctor.

If your child has a rash that is raised or puffy, it usually means there is a skin infection. However, a raised rash that is warm can mean fifth disease, which is not life-threatening. A raised rash on the face and neck can mean the measles. The best course of action if you are wondering about the rash is to simply ask your doctor.

Miscellaneous problems

There are other problems you should be aware of. If your child develops any of these, you should get medical attention as quickly as is possible.

- If your child is coughing up or vomiting blood, or has bloody diarrhea, this can be the sign of intestinal problems and must be immediately handled. This is especially true if your child has a fever at the same time.

- If your child is experiencing constant abdominal pain and is having trouble moving.

- If your child is having a seizure and does not have epilepsy or other types of seizure disorders.

- Testicular pain.

- If your child has suffered a head injury and has lost consciousness, or has begun to act differently than usual. If he or she is acting lethargic and not moving much after hitting his or her head, take the child to the doctor.

- Any cuts and scrapes that need stitches, as well as deep wounds or constant bleeding.

- If your child cannot swallow or breathe because of a severe allergic reaction.

- If your child has a severe headache that does not go away and is accompanied by vomiting and fever.

- If your child is at a healthy weight, but is losing weight. Any weight loss in a normally-proportioned child is not normal. It is often a sign that something is more seriously wrong with your child.

If you think you should take your child to the doctor, feel free to do so. You will not be the first or last father to worry too much about the cough your child has, so do not feel bad for taking your children to the doctor. It just shows you care and want them to be healthy.

CHAPTER CONCLUSION

One of the toughest jobs a father has is being the doctor. It is hard to be the doctor to your children when you are worrying about them getting better. You do not want to see your children sick. You do not want to see them throwing up or constantly coughing. It can be a hard thing to watch, but it is just a part of growing up. Your children will get sick, and when they do, they will worry you. All you can do is prepare yourself by learning what you can about childhood illnesses and preparing your home so you can help your children to the best of your ability if something does happen.

The great thing is that your children will generally not be sick often. If you can provide them with a happy, stress-free atmosphere where they eat well and are well-loved, they will grow up to be healthy and strong. Being Dr. Dad is not always easy, but when you help nurse your children back to health, it can be rewarding.

9 Cook

> *"Parenting is an impossible job at any age."*
>
> — Harrison Ford, American actor

Perhaps one of the toughest jobs a single father has is being the cook. While there are many men out there who can cook like a five-star chef, there are also many men who do not cook beyond toast, pizza, and cereal. This is fine when you are cooking for yourself, but when you are cooking for children, you need to put more care and consideration into cooking. You need to make sure your children get all the nutrients and minerals they need to grow up healthy. Cooking proper meals for your children and teaching them about nutrition can be one of the best things you ever do for your children.

THE RIGHT STUFF

If you are going to cook for your children, you need the right items in the kitchen to cook properly. If you went through a divorce, chances are you do not have much in your kitchen anymore beyond a microwave and toaster.

Items to purchase include:

1. Frying pan that is at least 10 inches in diameter

2. Saucepan with a cover

3. Wok

4. Strainer

5. Cookie sheet

6. Roasting pan that measures at least 9 by 11 inches

7. Measuring cups and spoons

8. Toaster oven

9. Slow cooker

10. Oven mitts

11. Assortment of mixing bowls

12. High-quality knives for cutting and preparing meals

13. Carving board

14. Spoons

15. Forks

16. Spatula

17. Mugs

18. Cups

19. Plates

20. Glasses

21. Small plates and bowls

22. Tupperware food storage containers

In consideration for your children, make sure to have special items in the kitchen, including:

1. Cups for children that are small enough to hold. Spill-proof cups are essential for smaller children.

2. Smaller plates that feature children's designs and cartoon characters.

3. Cookie cutters that the children can use to make cookies into interesting and fun shapes.

4. Smaller utensils for younger children.

Once you have most of these items, you can begin making your children wonderful meals that will have them coming back for seconds.

JAY KOEBELE

Jay R. Koebele
www.MyFrugalFather.com
Twitter: @jaykoebele
Email: jay1971@sbcglobal.net
Phone: 620-262-7174

I met my ex-wife online while in California, where I worked in the entertainment and music industries. Our relationship developed and I moved in with her and my two stepdaughters, going from bachelor to instant dad and husband. My son was born shortly thereafter, and my ex-wife and I raised our family over the next six years. As a family, we lived in Winfield, a town of less than 15,000 people located about 50 miles south of Wichita, Kansas.

My wife and I got divorced after being married for six years. We grew apart, our relationship became unhealthy, arguments became more frequent, and we were not enjoying our time together with each other. We tried counseling, but both realized we would be better parents to our children if we were divorced. It has been two years since we have separated, and over a year since our divorce, and we are better friends to this day.

Our parenting schedule is as follows: I have my son with me every other weekend, and I get time with my stepdaughters every other weekend, as well. The anticipation and excitement when I am preparing to spend time with my children is a wonderful feeling. I cherish every second that I am with my kids. I also enjoy being able to talk on the phone with them, discussing fun times we had last week or month.

On the cooking front, I refer to basic cookbooks and Web sites so I can come up with new things to prepare for my kids. It is important for me that the kids are exposed to a wide variety of foods. I realize, at times, they might not be interested in eating certain foods, especially if they have never had them or have pre-conceived notions of them.

But, as long as they are willing to taste or try them, I am fine with it. I realize kids go through phases with eating foods, and I know I was a picky eater up until high school. So, I do my best not to force anything on them. I hear many stories of parents who are dealing with teenagers' eating disorders, so the last thing I want to do is make my kids feel like they are not in control of their bodies and what they put in them.

It is important for them to feel like they are in control. I also happen to be a vegetarian.

My kids have known me as a vegetarian, but I do not force it on them. They ask me a lot of questions about why I am, and I tell them that I just prefer to not eat meat because I do not like the taste. Because my stepdaughters are 'tweens, they are old enough to hear that I do not like the way some animals are treated.

The best advice I can give is to be there for your kids. When you are with them, make them feel like you are giving them 100 percent, undivided attention. If you share parenting time and they are with their mom, make sure to give them space, but let them know you are there for them.

My Frugal Father

THE FOOD PYRAMID

Planning good meals for your children means that you should look at the tried-and-true food pyramid for inspiration. The food pyramid will help guide you to make meals that incorporate what your children need to eat to be and grow up healthy. We all know what the food pyramid looks like, but it is more important to talk about the individual parts of the pyramid and how each affect your children.

Grain

Grain is important for your children and typically comes in the varieties of bread, oatmeal, cereal, rice, and pasta. In the food pyramid, grain is listed in terms of ounces that should be served. To help, the following is a handy guide for ounces and grains.

Each of the following items equals 1 ounce:

- One slice of whole wheat bread
- Half a cup of oatmeal (available in whole wheat)
- Half a cup of rice (available in brown, which is whole wheat)
- Half a cup of pasta (available in whole wheat)
- One cup of cereal

Depending on the age of your children, they should eat the following servings of grains:

- Ages 2 to 8: 4 to 5 ounces of grain per day
- Ages 9 to 13 (girls): 5 ounces of grain per day
- Ages 9 to 13 (boys): 6 ounces of grain per day
- Ages 14 plus (girls): 6 ounces of grain per day

- Ages 14 plus (boys): 7 ounces of grain per day

It is important that the grain you do buy is not bleached or white. Buy your children whole grain items, like whole wheat bread and brown rice.

Vegetables

Vegetables are important, but are surprisingly not eaten much by many children. In the food pyramid, each vegetable serving is measured in cups. Depending on the age of your child, he or she will need a different amount of vegetables to be healthy:

- Ages 4 to 8: 1½ cups of vegetables per day
- Ages 9 to 13 (girls): 2 cups of vegetables per day
- Ages 9 to 13 (boys): 2½ cups of vegetables per day
- Ages 14 plus (girls): 2½ cups of vegetables per day
- Ages 14 plus (boys): 3 cups of vegetables per day

Fruits

Like vegetables, fruits are an important part of any healthy diet for children. As their father, you need to make sure your children get the recommended amount of fruits per day. Fruits are also measured in cups:

- Ages 4 to 8: 1 cup of fruit per day
- Ages 9 to 13: 1½ cups of fruit per day
- Ages 14 plus (girls): 1½ cups of fruit per day
- Ages 14 plus (boys): 2 cups of fruit per day

Milk and dairy

Healthy children need dairy to grow strong bones that will help them out through life. It is very important to ensure that your children get enough dairy each day to help the growth process. Give your children the following quantities of dairy daily:

- Ages 1 to 4: 1½ cups of milk/dairy per day
- Ages 4 to 8: 2 cups of milk/dairy per day
- Ages 9 to 13: 3 cups of milk/dairy per day
- Ages 14 plus: 3 cups of milk/dairy per day

Other dairy products can include yogurt and cheese. One cup of milk or yogurt equals 2 ounces (1/3 of a cup shredded) or 2 cups of cottage cheese.

Meat, poultry, fish, beans, and nuts

Your children will need iron and other proteins to grow and stay healthy. This is why you also need to make sure your children get the right amount of protein in their diets. As with grain, these protein foods are measured in ounces. One ounce equals:

- 1 ounce of meat, fish, or poultry
  (one ounce is roughly half a fist in size)
- ¼ cup of dry beans
- 1 egg
- 1 tablespoon of peanut butter
- ½ ounce of nuts or seeds

Each child needs the following amount of protein-rich foods in their diet:

- Ages 1 to 3: 2 to 3 ounces per day

- Ages 4 to 8: 3 to 4 ounces per day

- Ages 9 to 13: 5 ounces per day

- Ages 14 plus (girls): 5 ounces per day

- Ages 14 plus (boys): 6 ounces per day

By sticking to the food pyramid and avoiding other types of foods, you can help your children grow up healthy and ready to tackle life. As the rate of childhood obesity rises — currently at 15 percent for kids between the ages of six and 11 — it is important that parents work hard to not only help their children eat right, but also eat right themselves by setting the proper example as a role model.

Some foods you should only give to your children on special occasions include:

1.   Any type of take-out or fast food. Fast food in general should be avoided because it is high in trans fat, salt, and sugar.

2.   Limit the amount of salt your children ingest. Many children get far too much salt in their diets.

3.   Processed foods can also be a problem, as they have high amounts of trans fat and are not as healthy as fruits and vegetables.

4.   Junk food is obviously not good. Keep your children from eating too many chips and chocolate bars. If they need snacks, prepare fruit platters for them that are much healthier, cheaper, and just as filling.

The amount of sugar children currently eat is phenomenal. According to the U. S. Department of Agriculture, each child consumed about 12 pounds of sugar per year in the 1800s. By the 1970s, each child was eating 118 pounds per year, and by the 1990s, they were each eating 154 pounds per year. This essentially translates to each child eating 53 teaspoons of sugar per day. Each child should have no more than 6 to 18 teaspoons per day, at most. It is important to look at the sugar content of things like granola bars. Generally, one teaspoon equals 0.16 ounces. Here is the sugar content of some popular kid foods:

Hershey candy	1 bar	7 tsp sugar/1.10 ounces
Chewing gum	1 stick	½ tsp sugar/0.08 ounces
Chocolate cream	1 piece	2 tsp sugar/0.30 ounces
Butterscotch chew	1 piece	1 tsp sugar/0.20 ounces
Chocolate mints	1 piece	23 tsp sugar/3.80 ounces
Fudge	1 square	4¼ tsp sugar/0.70 ounces
Life Savers	1	1/3 tsp sugar/0.13 ounces
Donut (plain)	1	34 tsp sugar/5.70 ounces
Chocolate milk	1 8-oz glass	6 tsp sugar/1.0 ounce
Soft drinks	1 bottle	9 tsp sugar/1.5 ounces
Canned fruit juice (sweet)	½ cup	3 to 4 tsp sugar/0.50 to 0.70 ounces
Apricots, dried	4 to 6 halves	4 tsp sugar/0.70 ounces
White bread	1 slice	3 tsp sugar/0.50 ounces
Hamburger bun	1 whole bun	3 tsp sugar/0.50 ounces
Corn flakes	1 bowl	3 to 4 tsp sugar/0.50 to 0.70 ounces
Cheerios	1 bowl	3 to 4 tsp sugar/0.50 to 0.70 ounces
Wheaties	1 bowl	3 to 4 tsp sugar/0.50 to 0.70 ounces

VITAMINS AND MINERALS KIDS NEED

Since children grow so quickly and are developing so rapidly, it is very important that they have all the vitamins and minerals that they need to be healthy. As a father, knowing what minerals and vitamins your children need can help you plan better meals for them that take these needs into account. As a note, remember that young women need more iron, calcium, and Vitamin D at the onset of puberty.

Vitamin A

Vitamin A is very important and if your children do not have enough, they can develop a Vitamin A deficiency. At the same, time giving too much Vitamin A can be harmful. Roughly 200,000 to 500,000 children go blind each year because they have a severe Vitamin A deficiency. Some foods that are a source of Vitamin A include:

Milk	Liver
Sweet potatoes	Carrots
Broccoli	Butter (in small quantities)
Spinach	Leafy vegetables
Pumpkin	Spinach
Cantaloupe	Eggs
Apricots	Papaya
Mango	Peas
Winter squash	

Vitamin C

Vitamin C is essential to help prevent colds and aid against upper respiratory tract infections. If children have too little Vitamin C, it can lead to scurvy. While uncommon, scurvy is still found in some parts of the world. Too much Vitamin C can cause indigestion and diarrhea. Sources of Vitamin C include:

Liver	Pork
Lamb	Milk
Red peppers	Parsley
Broccoli	Brussels sprouts
Papayas	Strawberries
Oranges	Lemons
Cantaloupe	Cauliflower
Garlic	Grapefruit
Raspberries	Tangerines
Spinach	Cabbage
Lime	Mangos
Potatoes	Cranberries
Tomatoes	Pineapples
Grapes	Plums
Watermelons	Bananas
Carrots	Peaches
Apples	Asparagus
Pears	Lettuce

Iron

Iron is very important for children's growth to develop strong bones and muscles. It also improves the production of blood in the body. Choosing foods that are high in iron can greatly aid your child's development. To properly deal with oxygen in the body, iron is needed to aid cells that transport oxygen throughout the body. Sources of iron include:

Liver	Clams
Oysters	Oatmeal
Soybeans	Tofu
Lentils	Chickpeas
Beef	Shrimp
Pasta	Beans
Potatoes	Spinach
Pork/ham	Crab
Salmon	Eggs
Split peas	Raisins
Figs	Dates
Almonds	Cashews
Nuts	

Calcium

Your children need calcium in their bones to help them grow stronger. Having a diet rich in calcium can help your children grow with better bones, and can prevent osteoporosis later in life. Sources of calcium include:

Milk	Almonds
Sesame seeds	Beans
Oranges	Figs
Green vegetables	Broccoli
Soy milk	

Vitamin K

When your children hurt themselves, they may bleed. In order for blood to clot properly, children need to have enough Vitamin K in their diet. Vitamin K is often forgotten as parents focus on vitamins A, C, and D. However, low Vitamin K levels has been associated with osteoporosis and coronary heart disease. Sources of Vitamin K include:

Spinach	Cabbage
Cauliflower	Broccoli
Brussels sprouts	Avocados
Kiwi fruit	Parsley
Vegetable oil	Soybeans

Vitamin D

Vitamin D is extremely important for children. A lack of Vitamin D can lead to problems in both childhood and adulthood. Some of the problems that can be created by a Vitamin D deficiency include:

- Rickets, which is a disease that impedes growth and causes deformity in the bones

- Osteomalacia, which causes thinning bones, making them fragile

- Osteoporosis, which is a bone disease that can lead to fractures and a general brittleness of the bones

- High blood pressure

- Cancer

- Seasonal affective disorder, which is a condition that is most common during winter months and causes individuals to become depressed due to reduced sunlight

- Cognitive impairment, which is a difficulty concentrating, focusing and thinking

- Memory loss

- Autoimmune diseases, which are conditions that cause the immune system to get overactive and attack its own cells

- Type two diabetes, which is a form of autoimmune disease that requires insulin shots

The main source of Vitamin D is the sun, so it is important for children to spend time outdoors to get adequate sunlight. There are other sources of Vitamin D, some of which are dairy products fortified with Vitamin D. Common sources that naturally contain Vitamin D include:

Fish liver oils	Herring
Catfish	Salmon
Mackerel	Sardines
Tuna	Eggs
Beef liver	Swiss cheese

Zinc

For children, zinc plays an important role in development, especially as they become teenagers. Zinc helps the growth of children and plays a role in the sexual maturation of children and teens. Common sources of zinc include:

Beef	Lamb
Liver	Wheat
Bran	Sesame seeds
Poppy seeds	Celery
Mustard seeds	Alfalfa
Beans	Nuts
Almonds	Pumpkin seeds
Whole grains	Sunflower seeds

HOW MANY VITAMINS DO YOUR KIDS NEED EACH DAY?

By taking a look at the labels on the food you buy, you can see how many vitamins are in each meal you prepare for your children. Here is a handy guide for how many vitamins your children need.

Note: IU = International Units, which is the standard for measuring vitamin intake.

Vitamin A

- Ages 4 to 6: 2,500 IU
- Ages 7 to 14: 3,300 IU
- Ages 15 to 18 (boys): 5,000 IU
- Ages 15 to 18 (girls): 4,000 IU

Vitamin D

- Ages 4 to 6: 400 IU
- Ages 7 to 14: 400 IU
- Ages 15 to 18 (boys): 400 IU
- Ages 15 to 18 (girls): 400 IU

Vitamin E

- Ages 4 to 6: 9 IU
- Ages 7 to 14: 10 IU
- Ages 15 to 18 (boys): 15 IU
- Ages 15 to 18 (girls): 12 IU

Calcium

- Ages 4 to 6: 800 milligrams
- Ages 7 to 14: 800 milligrams
- Ages 15 to 18 (boys): 1,200 to 1,300 milligrams
- Ages 15 to 18 (girls): 1,200 to 1,300 milligrams

Iron

- Ages 4 to 6: 200 milligrams
- Ages 7 to 14: 250 milligrams
- Ages 15 to 18 (boys): 400 milligrams
- Ages 15 to 18 (girls): 300 milligrams

Zinc

- Ages 4 to 6: 10 milligrams
- Ages 7 to 14: 10 milligrams
- Ages 15 to 18 (boys): 15 milligrams
- Ages 15 to 18 (girls): 15 milligrams

PLANNING MEALS FOR KIDS

Now that you know what kids need to eat and the nutrients they need, you can get to meal planning. Meal planning involves creating a balance with minerals and nutrients children need, adding in protein, starch, vegetables, and fruits. It can be common for single fathers to make meals that are heavy on one aspect of the food pyramid, but not on others. Typically, you should have meals that balance the following:

- Protein

- o   Meat

- o   Fish

- o   Chicken

- o   Tofu or tempeh

- Starch

  - o   Potatoes

  - o   Rice

  - o   Barley

  - o   Pasta

  - o   Corn

  - o   Bread

- Vegetables

This means your children will get the iron and zinc they need from the protein part of the meal, while they will get their vitamins from the starch and vegetable portions of the meal.

One of the biggest problems that comes with planning meals for your children is getting them to actually eat what you make. Kids are known for not wanting vegetables, and it may be a power struggle for you to get your kids to eat vegetables or any healthy food. Picky eaters may be frustrating, but remain strong and focused. The harder you work to get them to eat right, the healthier they will be later. When you are planning the meals, use these tips to get kids to eat vegetables:

- Put peas in macaroni and cheese

- Add broccoli or spinach to pizza

- Add shredded carrots to tomato sauces that you put on pasta

- Bake shredded carrots, squash, and sweet potatoes into muffins and quick breads

- Add chopped-up vegetables to mashed potatoes or rice

- Put vegetables into the soups they like

- When you make hamburgers or meat loaf, add in minced vegetables

- Wrap vegetables in tacos, pitas, fajitas, and breads

- Make a burrito with mashed beans in it

- Melt cheese over cauliflower and broccoli

It may seem sneaky to do this, but it can serve an important purpose. Your kids will be eating vegetables, which is very important, but it also gives you leverage in the meal planning struggle. If you make a pizza and put broccoli on it, and a few days serve a meal with broccoli on the side, you may find your child does not want to eat the broccoli. At this point, tell him or her that he or she already ate it on the pizza and did not seem to have a problem with it.

Desserts can also be tricky, especially when you want your children to eat fruits instead of having chips or chocolate bars. Try to make the fruits more appealing for your children to eat. Instead of giving them apples on a plate, combine the apples with banana slices, put in some grapes, and top it off with low-fat yogurt. Or, top off some low-fat ice cream with strawberries or blueberries. Your kids may protest at first, but they will find these are actually a tasty desserts.

It is also important to watch the portions that your children eat. Since the 1970s, portion sizes have increased dramatically for both adults and children. As a result, children are eating more than ever before, but they seem to be eating less of the good stuff and more of the bad stuff. When you serve your children, keep an eye on how much they eat. Make sure they eat slowly. If you see food left over, or they are slowing down their eating but are still trying to get all the food off the plate, maybe you should lower their portion size.

GETTING HELP FROM THE KIDS

One common mistake made by fathers when preparing meals is not to get input or help from the kids. It is important as a father to include the kids in the meal preparation because you can help your children get interested in healthy eating by making cooking fun. Not all children want to take the time to cook, and that can lead to poor eating habits in adulthood. There are several reasons to include your children in meal planning, including:

- It helps their self-confidence by teaching them how to cook

- It gives them a skill they can use for years to foster a healthy diet in themselves

- It will encourage them to try new foods that they may not have previously been interested in

When you are planning meals with the kids, do the following:

1. Give the kids a pen and paper and let them write down foods they want for lunch or dinner. They will write down several good foods that you may not have thought about. What they write down can help you plan out good meals for all of you.

2. Take a look at their list and ask them questions about why they chose certain items. This can give you a window into what foods your children like and do not like, and why.

3. Go to the grocery store and have your children pick out the items they put on the list. Then, have them hand the cashier the money. This not only helps them learn to shop for food, but it also teaches the concept of money and paying for what we need.

Cooking dinner

Once you have planned meals with the kids, you can begin getting them to help you cook dinner. When you do this, it is important to have the kids start young, and important to make the entire process fun. If you make cooking a chore, they will not want to do it.

Follow these tips when you get help from the kids to cook dinner:

1. Start the kids off with baking. Generally, baking is easier than cooking, and kids will love being able to make treats for themselves and the family.

2. If your children are young, make things simple. If cooking is too complicated, they may lose interest and you will end up doing everything yourself. As they get older, make things more inventive.

3. To start, have the kids make snacks for the family. As time goes on and their skills improve, get them cooking breakfast on occasion, then lunch, and finally family dinners.

4. Weekends are the best time to have your kids work on cooking. They will not be as tired from school and will not have to do homework on a Saturday night.

DOING DISHES

Few children enjoying doing dishes, but it is important that they learn how to do them from a young age. Not only does this help you with everything you need to do around the house, but it also teaches your children the importance of keeping things clean. Talking to them about the dangers of leaving food on plates and how it can make people sick can save them suffering later on.

First, get your child a stepladder or small box so he or she can be level with the sink. You want to make it easy for your child to walk up to the sink. It is important to remember that he or she is not the only one doing dishes. You should be helping, especially at first. When you help, you make it fun for the kids, as well as a bonding experience for all of you.

Give your children their own sponges and scrubbers — make it something they can call their own. This makes doing dishes more fun because they are using their own. Start the kids off by rinsing the dishes. Make sure you look at each dish and explain to them why the dishes need to be rinsed off after they are in the sink, or before they go into the dishwasher.

To start, give your children easy-to-clean items that are not breakable. Let them wash the dish and ensure that it is clean. If it is not, show them the spots they missed and explain the importance of clean dishes. Once the dishes are all clean, have your kids help you wipe off and dry the counters and around the sink. It is up to you if you want your children to be rewarded for helping you, which can teach them the concept of working for money, or you can simply make it a reward of the value of hard work and your respect.

It is important to have your children help you with cleaning after supper. Many children forget that supper is not just about the food in front of them, but about the preparation and the cleanup afterwards. By doing dishes with your children, you are bonding with them and showing them that supper is not done until all the dishes are put away and the counters are cleaned off. Then it is time to relax, focus on homework, or have fun. In regards to what age you should start your children doing dishes, a good age is about eight years old. At this point, they know to be careful with dishes, and they will understand that helping around the house is important. Any younger age will require you to supervise extensively and make sure only certain dishes are washed by them. This can still be a good idea, since it makes having them wash the dishes at eight years old and older much easier.

CHAPTER CONCLUSION

One of the hardest roles for single fathers is that of a cook. Whether it is a stereotype, or if men are simply not good cooks, cooking for children can be a trying experience. However, cooking for children can also be a great bonding experience. When you work with your children to prepare and create meals for them, you are helping get them interested in healthy eating and cooking. These are skills and philosophies that can help them well into the future.

Cooking may not be your forte, but as a single father, it is what you need to do so your kids eat healthy.

10 Disciplinarian

> *"And in that time, I lost my dad and had kids of my own. It was like, OK, I get it now. I know what fatherhood is all about. And you look at your parents differently."*
>
> — Paul Reiser, American comedian and actor

One of the hardest roles for a single father to play is that of the disciplinarian. It can be hard to discipline the kids, especially if you only have limited time with them. Why would you want to be the bad guy when you have two days with them before they go back to their mother? Nonetheless, being the disciplinarian with your children when it is called for is important. Not only does it teach them respect for you, it also helps you teach your children to be upstanding members of society. It is obvious that a lack of discipline does not always breed well-adjusted adults.

COMMON PATTERNS

After a father has become divorced or widowed, and he is now required to administer discipline on his own, there are three patterns the father can fall into.

1. **The Friend:** With this pattern, the father wants to be the friend, rather than the authority figure. He will become more lenient with the children and rules will begin to slide. A common feeling can be guilt for getting mad at the children and telling them what to do. If a father has custody, he may worry that being too strict could cost him custody, while if he has partial custody, he feels competitive with the ex-spouse.

2. **The Drill Sergeant:** On the flip side, the father may become extremely strict. After a divorce, fathers can feel that they lost control, so being able to lay down the rules in a strict manner gives them more control. Often in this case, punishments can be severe for minor rule violations. An example would be no television for two months because of staying up too late.

3. **The Flip-Flopper:** This type of pattern is a combination of being a friend and being a drill sergeant. This is the most common pattern fathers can get into when they must deal with discipline. A common occurrence is being lenient about something for several months and then suddenly enforcing a rule with no warning to the kids. This is the worst pattern to have because it will set the kids on edge, and they will begin acting inconsistent, too.

WHEN TO ADMINISTER DISCIPLINE

When your children do not listen to you, there is obviously a need for discipline. However, this is not the only time you should enable discipline with your children. There are a multitude of reasons why discipline may be required:

- Your children ignore or disobey your instructions
- Your children talk or yell back at you
- Your children lash out at their siblings
- Your children break something they were not supposed to touch
- Your children refuse to do schoolwork
- Your children do not respect your authority

When it comes time to administer discipline, you need to be ready. You cannot waver and you have to be firm with your children. Although you are their father and can have fun with them, you are in charge — they should not try and challenge your authority by disobeying you.

SETTING RULES AND BOUNDARIES

You are going to need to establish rules and boundaries with your children. These are the limits of what you will allow your children to do. Remember to correlate boundaries with your ex-wife if you are divorced. Boundaries and rules can include:

- Bedtimes
- What can be watched on television
- What grades the children should attempt to obtain
- How much time should be spent on homework
- The chores that have to be done
- How much time can be spent on the computer/video game system

One mistake that many fathers make is creating rules and boundaries and not explaining them, or not attempting to show the kids why those rules are in place. To help your children understand why they need to have rules and boundaries, follow these steps:

1. First, consider the age of your children; their ages will affect the rules you put in place. An 8 p.m. bedtime for your 7-year-old is acceptable, but it is not for a 15-year-old. You should also remember that your children need to be independent and have their own individual personalities. You, as their father, need to balance allowing them to grow and develop, while putting in place boundaries and rules that protect them, not hinder them.

2. You need to talk to your kids about the rules and the boundaries before you implement them. Your children are intelligent, and if you talk to them about why some rules are into place, they will be more likely to follow those rules. Allow your children to understand the limitations you are putting in place and the consequences of not following those limits.

3. It is important that you take time for your children to understand the consequences of misbehaving. Be clear and completely outline the consequences of breaking the rules you have laid down.

4. For younger children, one good tip to help them remember the rules and boundaries you have set is to have a chart. A chart will spell out the rules in a way that your children will be able to understand. That way, you can use the chart as a way of keeping your children in line, as they

will know exactly what they are allowed and not allowed to do.

HOW TO DISCIPLINE PROPERLY

It is not always easy to discipline, and before delving into the methods of discipline, it is important to address how to do so. This is not about raising your voice, what to do with the children when they are bad, or whether or not you should spank. It is about how you can make discipline the most effective when laying down rules and boundaries for your children.

- Most of all, you need to be consistent. If you are not consistent, your children will not learn to follow the rules and boundaries. Think of it this way: If you sometimes got in trouble at work for showing up late, and other times your boss did not care, what would you do? You would most likely start showing up late more often because you know you can get away with it. Occasionally, you get in trouble, but you are more often than not getting off scot-free. If you are divorced, you should talk to your ex about the rules that will be implemented. The last thing you want are your children saying, "We can at Mom's house!" If they do, you need to tell them that this is your house and your rules will be followed.

- There have to be reasonable limits on your rules and boundaries. It is not reasonable to expect your children to never watch television, so do not put such a rule in place. Plus, reasonable limits show that you are the boss; your children need to know who is in charge in your house.

- There needs to be a link between bad behavior and the consequences. If your child stays out late and you take away the television, what is the link? If they stay out late and you ground them from going out, there is a clear link between what they did and the punishment they received. If children see the links between the punishment and the crime, they will be more likely to follow your rules.

- Probably the biggest worry fathers have about setting rules is that their children will stop loving them. There may be times when it seems it, but in the end they will always love you. Try to keep reasonable rules in place, otherwise you may actually drive your children away because of their need for freedom and individuality.

- When you are enforcing rules, make sure you give your children limited choices. An example of this is if your child refuses to get off the computer after he or she has exceeded the set time limit. In this case, you should say "Either you get off the computer now, or you lose the privilege for a week." Now you have given your child a choice, as well as a punishment that fits the crime.

- Understand that your children may be acting out or misbehaving for a reason. They do not want to just wildly flout the rules — they have a method to the madness. Generally, there are reasons for the behavior. These reasons can include:

  o Your children want you to give them attention. Often, this is the most common reason for their behavior.

o They want to challenge your authority and be in control. Whether you want to accept it or not, humans are social animals and need to have someone in control. If your child feels you are not doing a good job, he or she may instinctively want to take your job away from you.

o Your children want to get back at you. In this case, they feel you did something wrong to them and want to get back at you for it. If you sent them to bed without supper because they swore at you, they may break something the next day because they are upset.

o They are frustrated. This can be a harder reason to see, but if you do see that your child is frustrated, find out the reason so the two of you can talk about and work through it.

DEALING WITH BAD BEHAVIOR

When your child acts out, you need to address it. There are many ways to do this. In the past, one of the most common methods to deal with bad behavior was spanking. There are parents who feel that spanking is corporal punishment and should never be used. On the other hand, there are parents who feel that spanking is a fine punishment for children who misbehave. The choice is up to you as the parent.

Some studies that support the claim against spanking are:

• In 1996, a study conducted by Straus, Sugarman, and Giles-Sims found that children who received spanking as a punishment were likely to use spanking as a punishment when they were adults. Those same children were also more angry and more approving of hitting a spouse.

- In 1997, another study by Straus, Sugarman, and Giles-Sims found that spanking frequently caused detrimental effects to children, including low-self esteem. However, there are researchers who feel that there is no harm in the occasional spanking of a child in the long run.

Some studies that support the claim for spanking are:

- In 1996, a study conducted by Robert Larzelere, a Ph.D. at the Nebraska Medical Center, found that spanking in some instances increases compliance with the authority and commands of the parents.

- Diana Baumrind, a clinical and development psychologist, has done studies that open-hand spanking from the parent is unlikely to have a severe detrimental effect on the child.

How to respond if...

- Your child is acting out for attention: In this case, you should make the decision to pay more attention to your child, but avoid giving him or her special treatment. You should tell your child that if he or she acts out, there will be consequences. Remember to create a link between the crime and the punishment. Make sure your child knows that you love him or her and try and find ways to redirect his or her behavior.

- Your child wants to take control: In this case, you should talk with your child and find out if he or she can find a solution to the problem with you. Do not enter into a conflict with your child, but make sure you immediately follow through with any punishment. Be firm with your child and give him or her limited choices as to how he or she wants to progress after exhibiting that behavior.

- Your child is getting even with you: In this case, do not have retaliation on your mind, but let your child know how you are feeling and encourage him or her to talk to you when there is something wrong.

- Your child is frustrated: In this case, show your child that you believe in him or her and believe he or she can achieve anything. Do not criticize your child, and be sure to praise him or her when he or she does something positive. A Florida-based study by Kathryn Kvols, president of the International Network for Children and Families, found that the average child gets 400 negative comments a day, but only 32 positive. This is something to change with your children if you want them to keep from feeling frustrated. Do not feel sorry for your child, but try to put him or her in environments where he or she can succeed and gain self-esteem.

Acceptable forms of punishment (pre-teen years)

One excellent form of punishment is to have your child sit in a corner. This has been used for decades as punishment and is effective. Designate an area of your home as the time-out area. To do the time-out effectively, remember to always stay calm and in control of your emotions. Follow these instructions:

1. First, remove your child from what is causing the misbehavior. If he or she is doing it for attention, it is good to get him or her away from everyone.

2. You want him somewhere with no stimulation. Sending your child to his or her room does not always work because the child is comfortable there and likes his or her room. Time-out is a punishment, not a time to relax.

3. In a firm voice, without yelling, tell your children they are misbehaving and that they are going to sit in the time-out area until you say they can come out.

4. A good rule of thumb is to have your child stay in the time-out area for every year of his or her age. This means that if your child is two, he or she should stay in time-out for two minutes. If he or she is five, have him or her stay for five minutes.

5. When the time-out is over, have your child apologize for his or her behavior.

6. If your child does not apologize, he or she needs to go back into the time out area.

7. If your child continues to refuse to apologize, send him or her to his or her room for the rest of the night. However, when you send the child to his or her room, remove toys, the television, video game systems, or books so he or she is not having fun when he or she is supposed to be punished. If the child refuses to obey the time-out and keeps coming out of his or her room, be persistent. This can sometimes go on for an hour or more before the child

stays in the room. If you are not consistent or give up, you lose a portion of your authority.

Another form of effective punishment is to remove privileges. If your child likes to go to the park every day, remove that privilege if he or she stays at the park longer than what you allow. If he or she watches television past his or her bedtime, take away the right to watch television for a specified period of time.

Occasionally, warnings will be more useful than a punishment. If your child is misbehaving while you are having dinner, warning him or her that he or she may lose dessert is more effective than taking the dessert away immediately. Warnings can be used if you want to give your child a chance to behave, as well. If he or she does not heed the warning, implement the punishment and say, "You were warned," or, "Make good choices."

Acceptable forms of punishment (teenage years)

Putting your teenager in a corner as a punishment is not going to be effective, so you need a new list of ways to punish when you are dealing with teenagers. To punish your teenage children, try the following ideas:

1. It is best to think about what your teen finds important, and use that as leverage in a punishment. For example, if he or she enjoys driving, take away the car keys. If he or she likes to talk on the cell phone, have the cell phone service limited so that only you can be called in case of emergency. Some parents even give their teenagers only a few minutes on the cell phone per day if they have misbehaved.

2. Take away your teenager's favorite things, including the television, leisure computer time, and the video game system. If he or she uses the Internet a lot, take away the Internet by password protecting the browser.

3. Restrict access to friends. Friends are important to teenagers, so by not allowing friends over for a period of time or grounding your teenager, you can take away something that really matters to him or her. You can cut into your teen's social life by not allowing him or her to go to school functions where he or she may see friends. Essentially, your teen goes to school and comes home, that is it.

4. If you give your teenager an allowance, you can dock him or her money for the misbehavior.

5. You can have your teenager do hard time by giving him or her extra chores around the house to pay the debt for misbehaving. If your teenager enjoys sleeping in, wake him or her up early to do chores.

6. If you really want to scare your teenager straight, tell him or her that if he or she does not listen to you, you will drive him or her to school every day for a month, while wearing your pajamas.

BEING A FRIEND

It is important to provide structure to your children by ensuring that you are in charge, and that means taking on the role of disciplinarian. However, it is also important that you are a friend to your children. A friend does not just mean you only play with your children, laugh with them, and spend time together; it means that you listen to them, talk with them, and hear what is on their minds.

Friend or father

Some fathers feel that a father can only be a friend or a father, but not both. The father is in charge; he is the one who hands down rules and boundaries for the children. There is no room for a friend in this regard. However, without the father being a friend, children will have trouble bonding with him. You can simultaneously be a friend and father. The sooner you realize this, the sooner you can create a bond with your children where they love you as a friend and respect you as a father.

Creating the bond

The bond you create with your children as their friend is one that is very strong. This is important in later years when it is not quite as easy to get your children to listen to you. Create a bond with your children in the following ways:

- Play games with them
- Read with them
- Go for walks together
- Visit places like the zoo, movie theater, and miniature golf course
- Talk with them
- Help them with their extra-curricular activities
- Watch television with them, while discussing the message the program is sending
- Go on nature hikes with them

- Help them with their schoolwork
- Attend their sporting events, plays, and other events that matter to them

When you do these things with your children, they will begin to learn that you care and want to spend time with them. This is important because your children want to know their father is there for them. Whether you are a single father through divorce or widowhood, being a friend your children can rely on is something that cannot be understated in importance. If you only have joint custody, you want to make the most of your time with your children, and that means being a friend to them.

Activities with the children (baby to toddler)

- Toddlers are fascinated by a variety of things, and you can use that to create low-cost activities. Get some uncooked rice and cups, grab a funnel, and let the kids pour rice through the funnel and into another clear cup. As odd as it seems, toddlers seem to have a lot of fun with this simple activity.

- With some water-based paint that is safe for children, set up a large sheet of paper that both you and your child can use to make a painting. Make sure you have a variety of colors on hand and let your child paint with his or her fingers. You will both have a lot of fun, and this also helps fuel your child's creative ability.

- Building forts is fun for both you and your child. With cushions from the couch, boxes, and blankets, you can make an extensive fort in the living room. In the fort, you can read stories, have snacks, and play games.

Activities with the children (ages 2 to 10)

- Play board games with the kids. Board games come in many varieties for all ages. Pick a game that is right for your child's age, and you can both have a lot of fun with it. As time goes, on, choose more advanced board games. One good tip is to create a family game night. This can be any night of the week that works best for everyone. On game night, there is no television, just the kids' favorite foods and games. It is a great way to bond with your children.

- One idea some fathers never think about is taking their children on a date. These are fun dates where you take the children somewhere they like. It can be to a movie, the zoo, a museum, the library, a baseball game, anything they want. It can also be dinner at their favorite restaurant. This is a good idea because it gives your children time with you alone. There are no other worries during family date night.

- Scavenger hunts are fun for all ages, and they can give your children much-needed exercise. One type of scavenger hunt is known as geocaching. It involves using GPS receivers to find hidden containers. The coordinates are revealed to those who belong to groups on the Internet. This is a good way to spend time in the outdoors with the children.

Activities with the 'tweens' (11 to 13)

- If your children are avid readers, read with them. Even if it means sitting out on the deck and reading books together, it can be an important bonding experience.

- You can use some of the previously mentioned activities with 'tweens, including:

  o Board games and a family game night

  o Dates out to places your children enjoy

  o Scavenger hunts

- Crafts are fun and can help your children be creative. The Internet has dozens of crafts Web sites. Whether it is feather bookmark or milk jug bird feeders, you can enjoy making some great crafts with your 'tweens. Some places to look for crafts include:

  o **www.allcrafts.net**

  o **www.allfreecrafts.com**

  o **www.marthastewart.com**

- If there is a concert your 'tween wants to go to, go with him or her. Even if you are not a big fan of the band or artist playing, you can still go and show support with your child.

- Your child may be wanting to see a certain movie, and a good way to bond with him or her is to go with and show an interest in it. You may not want to see the movie, but it is important to show an interest in what your 'tween is into at that moment.

- If your 'tween is a fan of a certain sport, take him or her to a game. You can also talk to your child about enrolling in the sport.

Activities for teenagers

1. If you are fixing something around the house, get your teenager involved. It is a good time to bond, and you are teaching them a life skill they can use in the future. Both your son and daughter can take part in something like this.

2. Teenagers have a lot of energy, and a good outlet for can be sports. Whether you are playing catch with your daughter or soccer with your son, you can bond by playing sports together.

3. An excellent bonding activity is teaching your teenagers to drive. Once they have a learner's permit, you can begin driving with them. The age a person can obtain a permit differs for each state. Check the online Unofficial DMV Guide at: **www.dmv.org/**. This is also important because you are teaching your teenager to drive in a safe manner.

4. There is no reason why you cannot have a family game night, although depending on your teenager's social life, it may have to be done during the week as opposed to a Friday or Saturday.

5. If you are building something like a new shed, table, or bookshelf, you can get your teenager involved, too.

The danger of spoiling

When you are a single father, especially if you do not see your children very often, you may fall into the trap of spoiling. Spoiling involves buying your children gifts and presents, praising them excessively, and generally being more of a friend than a father to them.

Spoiling is defined as:

- Not enforcing consistent limits
- Shielding a child from everyday frustrations
- Excessive gifts given no matter the circumstances, and even when the child has misbehaved

If your child is under the age of six months, there is nothing wrong with spoiling. As long as your child does not associate crying with getting attention, there is no problem. Once your child reaches the age of 18 months, but before three years, start placing limits. Your child will test the limits, but you should remain firm and not spoil excessively during this age range. Many parents feel guilty if they do not give their children what they want, especially toys and attention, during this phase. After the age of three, there should be restrictions on how many material things the children are given. The last thing you want is to be a "Disneyland Dad," where you give the children whatever they want whenever you see them. They will love what you provide for them, but may not love you specifically. A spoiled child can develop the following traits:

- Anger over not getting what he or she wants — the child will be annoyed and feel mistreated
- Difficulty making friends
- Employment problems
- Personal relationship problems

- Anger problems
- Professional problems

No different than being a friend to your children, you also need to help them with their schooling. School is not always easy, and having a father who helps with homework can mean a lot to your children.

BEING A TEACHER

Hopefully you remember how to do algebra, because as a father, another role you assume is that of a teacher. As their father, your kids will come to you for help with their homework, so you need to be there to help them. Because your kids spend a lot of time at school, they may also want you to help out with school programs. By making yourself part of that life, you can help forge a stronger bond with them over the years they are in school.

Talking to teachers

After your divorce or the death of your wife, schedule a meeting with teachers to let them know about the changing dynamic in the family, and to assure them that you will be there to help your children through school. If you are a single father, it is important to take an active role in school with your children. It can be hard when you work, but create a balance so you can spend time at your child's work, which is school.

Some things to talk to teachers about include:

1. Participating in parent-teacher conferences

2. Sports programs

3. After-school activities

4. School events, like pageants and plays

Tell the teachers you would like a copy of your child's report card so you can see how he or she is doing. This is usually not a problem, and most teachers will be happy to help out a father who is taking an active interest in his child's schooling. You can even have the

report cards e-mailed to you directly. Depending on the school your children go to and the policies of that school, you may be required to sign the report cards, so you will see the cards no matter what.

Helping with homework

Helping your children with their homework is not just about going through problems with them, it is about creating a setting in which they can complete homework. It is about making homework fun; something easy they can do. You should do the following when helping your children with homework.

1. Set a regular time for your children to finish any homework assignments. You want to schedule a time that works for both you and your children. It also depends on the age of your child. Younger children may work better on homework after playing in the afternoon, while older children may work better after dinner. You should not have your children doing homework past 9 p.m. When you do create a schedule, put it somewhere visible, like on the refrigerator door.

2. Children also need a place to do homework. You want a study area that has light, supplies, and solitude. A desk

in a study or bedroom is great, but you can also use part of the living room or the kitchen table. Let your children decorate their study corner — it will make it a much happier atmosphere for them to do homework.

3.   Your children need supplies when they do homework, so provide them with what they need, including:

- Pencils
- Pens
- Erasers
- Paper
- Dictionary
- Paper clips
- Calculator
- Sharpener
- Tape
- Scissors
- Ruler
- Thesaurus
- Almanac
- Stapler
- Folders

4.   You need to be an example to your children. When they are studying or doing homework, lead by example. Instead of watching television while they do homework, read. Take them to educational places like museums and zoos, or play educational games with them. Children

learn from their parents, so if they see you learning, they will want to do the same.

5.   You spend a lot of time around your children, so it should not be too hard for you to learn how your children learn best. By talking with them, you will be able to find out how they learn.

- If you find your child learns best when he or she can see something, use drawings and charts.

- If your child learns best through hearing, use stories and spoken directions.

- If your child learns by handling items, you can help by using props. For example, help your child learn about fractions by cutting up an apple or a pie.

6.   You can help your child prepare for tests by giving him or her practice tests, and then correcting the tests.

Praise is important

Your children want to know they are doing a good job, and it is important that you praise your children when they are doing homework. This does not mean telling them they did a good job when they thought $2 + 2 = 7$. However, it is important to show encouragement by saying "You were close with that one, but now we will work together to get the right answer." When your child finishes his or her homework or does a book report, read it and him or her them what you think. Say, "Good job on the first draft of the report, I think you really have a good foundation." If your children think they are doing a good job, they are going to be more willing to work hard in the future.

Do not be rude or overbearing with your children, as this will only cause them to get frustrated. Encouragement is incredibly important when you are helping children with homework.

CHAPTER CONCLUSION

It can be hard to not spoil a child, or to discipline them, but it is important for parents to balance the line between discipline and friendship. On the one hand, you need to enforce rules and boundaries, but on the other, you need to allow kids to be kids and let them have fun.

It can be difficult at first to develop a balance, but as time goes on you will begin to see when you need to be the father and when you need to be the friend. Once you reach that point, you will find that you develop a good relationship with your children where you are both a role model and a friend. You are there to help them through problems they may have on their homework, and to help them solve some of the mysteries of life.

Teacher, friend, and disciplinarian, are many of the different hats that a father must wear.

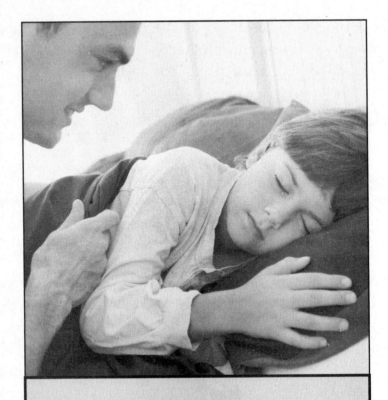

"Children make you want to start life over."

— Muhammad Ali, American althlete

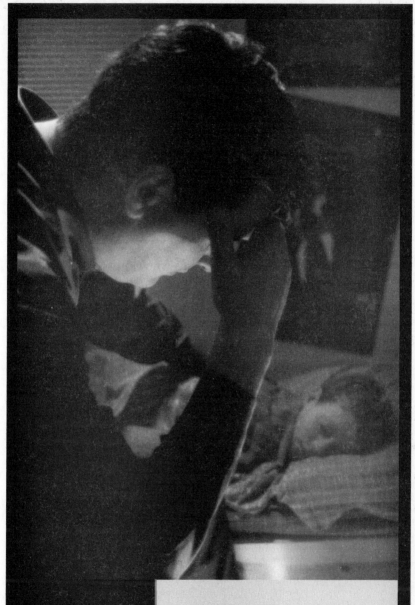

4

Meeting The Challenges

"Father taught us that opportunity and responsibility go hand in hand. I think we all act on that principle; on the basic human impulse that makes a man want to make the best of what's in him and what's been given him."
— Laurence Rockefeller, venture capitalist

11 Dealing With A Son

> *"My father used to play with my brother and me in the yard. Mother would come out and say, "You're tearing up the grass;" "We're not raising grass," Dad would reply. "We're raising boys."*
>
> — Harmon Killebrew, Hall of Fame baseball player

Often, it can be easier for a father to raise a son than a daughter because they can relate to each other. That does not mean it is easy: Sons can be high-energy, injury-prone, and aggressive at times. With a son, there is also the need to be a role model, where the father teaches the son what it is to be a man. There are many challenges to a father who is raising a son. These include puberty, dating, providing outlets for energy, and more. However, there can be a strong bond created with a father and son when they take part in activities together and talk with each other, sharing emotions. Being the single father of one or more boys can be an amazing journey, with only a few bumps in the road.

WHAT TO EXPECT

With a son, there are several things to expect while they are growing up. These are true for most boys, but will come in varying degrees. For example, while all boys will get scraped knees, only some will break bones. While most boys will have some aggression, only a small percentage will have problems with it. Some of the things you will go through with your son are the following:

- Your son will get injured, but to differing degrees

- Your son will have a lot of energy, and you will need to find outlets for it

- Your son will want to roughhouse and will have aggression, which is something you will need to deal with properly

- Your son will go through puberty, which can be a trying time for a single father

- Your son will want to date, and you may have to put some rules in place

Injuries

According to Children's Hospital Boston, roughly three million children each year will be injured in sports and recreational activities. Interestingly, before puberty, girls are more likely to be injured, but after puberty, boys are more likely to be injured. Regardless of whether you have a son or daughter, teach him or her about wearing protective equipment and being smart when playing. If you have children in sports, protective equipment is essential, but you cannot have your son running around in a helmet when he is playing with friends. When your son plays outside, he may fall and hurt his arm, or may trip and break a tooth. It happens, and there are some things you cannot plan for. However, you should talk to your son about how to play smart and safe.

1. Teach your son that while it is fun to climb trees, climbing too high or on trees with thin limbs can be dangerous.

2. Teach your son about playing safe around traffic. Everyone knows to watch for the ball followed by a child running out in the street, but you can prevent that from happening by showing the danger that your son faces in the street.

3. Roughhousing is fine, but show your son that he must be careful when playing aggressively. Tell him that rough-housing on the grass is fine, but roughhousing at the top of a slide is not.

It is important to not become over-protective with your children and their playing. The current generation of children spend a lot of time indoors, and many parents do not want their children playing outside unsupervised because they worry their children will be injured.

Boys will be boys and may get injured — it is part of growing up. You cannot place your children in bubble wrap, but you can show them how to be safe when they play. Teaching your son how to play safe is important, because then you can allow him to play at the park in a pick-up game of baseball, or play tag in the backyard.

Energy

All children have a lot of energy. This is something you should prepare for. They may run around screaming, for example, especially after eating something sugary. This is normal. Kids are going to have energy, but if you do not channel it in constructive ways, such as sports or active games, it could result in injury or misbehavior.

Aggression

Where aggression comes from is up for debate. Many believe video games and television help spur aggression in boys, while others feel it is something inherent in everyone. Regardless, aggression may be something you have to deal with. If your son is aggressive, it usually means there is an exterior circumstance causing it. Sometimes it could be a problem with self-esteem that causes him to lash out, or it could be a need for attention.

Like with energy, find an outlet for aggression. The most commonly used outlet for aggression in boys is sports. Sports allow for the sense of competition that is inherent in men in a controlled atmosphere. This will allow an outlet for both energy and aggression, and helps teach important lessons about life and working with others.

DEALING WITH PUBERTY

Puberty is something you will expect from your children, but it can be difficult to deal with, especially if you are a single father. Your son is going to have a lot of questions, and because you went through the same thing, you should not have too much trouble answering them. However, it is good to prepare yourself for the questions so your son can go into puberty understanding what is changing with his body. If you need help answering some of your son's questions, you can find a wealth of information on these Web sites.

- Young Men's Health (**www.youngmenshealthsite.org**): Health information, sexuality and dating, nutrition, acne, fitness, and emotional health are all covered here. There is even a blog about relevant topics in teenagers' lives, such as college, camping trips, and dating. Research this Web site, along with others, to have all the answers to your son's questions.

- U.S. Department of Health (**www.hhs.gov**): Go to this Web site, click the "Families" tab, then click "Teenage Health" under the "Teens" heading. Information about depression, alcohol, sexually transmitted diseases, specific female hormone issues, sexual health, the Human Papilloma Virus vaccine, and more topics are included.

- WebMD (**www.webmd.com**): This Web site has myriad pages of information about any health-related question you may have about puberty or other issues.

Changing classmates

One of the first things your son may ask you about is why the girls in his class are getting taller. Girls usually start growing between the ages of eight and 13, whereas boys do not start until a year or two after that. You can talk to your son and tell him the girls are going through puberty, as he will too. Tell your son that he will begin growing soon and will most likely become taller than the girls as time goes on. If he is worried about growing tall, you can tell him about the importance of a healthy diet and exercise, which can help the development process and help his body remain healthy through puberty.

Changing shape

Your son will begin to worry about his body as he begins to grow. One of the biggest concerns will be muscles. He may see his friends beginning to grow larger, and he may see muscles appearing on them. If he asks you why muscles have not started to show on him, you can tell him that puberty moves at its own schedule and his time will come. Your son can start to lift weights, but this will not create muscles — it will only tone those muscles he already has. Another option is to have your son eat healthy and be active in sports and outdoor activities. Your son may not want to talk about his changing shape or insecurities with his body, but there are signs you can look for. If your son spends a lot of time in front of the mirror looking at his body, it may be something he is insecure about. Also, if your son wears baggy clothes that hide his body, it could be a sign of insecurity. The best course of action is to talk with him and learn more about what is on his mind.

Thinking about girls

When your son is younger than 10 or so, he wants nothing to do with girls. Once puberty sets in, however, all he can think about are girls. This will seem odd to him. He will find he sweats around girls, thinks about them constantly, and will have trouble understanding what is happening to him. In this case, you should talk to your son and tell him that with puberty comes a growing awareness of girls, thanks to his burgeoning hormones. Tell him that as his hormones become more active, he will begin to have more emotions and feelings. These feelings can be confusing to a boy, and scary at times, but it is important that you explain it is a completely natural process for his body.

Hair growth

When your son begins to learn about puberty through talking with you or at school, he may become fixated on hair growth. Typically hair growth on the body will begin between the ages of 11 to 13. It is extremely common for boys to wake up every day to see if they are officially "a man." As they go through puberty, hair will begin to appear on their chin, cheeks, upper lip, chest, legs, armpits, and pubic region.

As the hormones from the pituitary gland spread through the body, they begin to make the testicles of boys grow bigger, which then causes a release of testosterone. The testosterone then causes hair to sprout all over the body. When you notice your son is beginning to have hair on his face, you may want to talk to him about shaving. While he may think that a 'teenage mustache' is cool, it is still up to you to show him the importance of shaving.

Body odor

To keep your son from being "the smelly kid" in class, talk to him about perspiration and body odor. Even though body odor was not a problem in the past, it will be during puberty. Generally, the body odor problem will begin around the age of 12. Some boys will start earlier with body odor, while others will start later. Either way, it will happen within one to two years of the age of 12. When your son's body becomes hotter than 98.6 degrees Fahrenheit, the body will begin to sweat; that sweat then turns to vapor to help cool us down. Sweat can have a bad smell to it, especially during and after puberty. The smell is caused by ammonia, salts, and sugar that are found in bacteria on the skin. As a result, when your son sweats, the vapor makes contact with the bacteria to cause the smell. This is a good time to introduce your son to deodorant. There are many types of deodorant, and it is best to let your son find the type he likes the most.

Erections

It can be hard to talk to your son about erections, but it can be a very strange change for your son to go through from his perspective. During puberty, erections can happen at nearly any time: day or night, in front of class, or while sitting on the couch while watching television. For a boy going through puberty, an erection can be incredibly embarrassing. It is important that you talk to your son and explain to him that erections happen and they are nothing to be embarrassed about. Keep in mind your son may not want to talk to you about this sensitive topic. It can be awkward for both of you, but you should not shy away from the topic. Your son will wonder why he is getting erections, and may worry something is wrong. School does a good job of explaining erections these days, but it can be important for your son to hear it from his father. Explain why they happen, as well as various ways to deal with them when they happen in a public setting, like school.

BONDING WITH YOUR SON

Raising a son by yourself creates the perfect opportunity to bond with him. There are many ways to bond with your son, but for a father, the best ways are spending time with him, participating in sports, and finding common interests.

The previous section included activities fathers can enjoy with their children. It is important to find an activity that both you and your son enjoy for the two of you to properly bond. If your son is young and enjoys playing with trucks, play trucks with him. If your son enjoys drawing, draw with him. It is easier to find things to do with your son by knowing what he likes to do, rather than force your son to like what you do. That does not mean you cannot introduce him to things you like, but do not take it personally if he does not get as into it as you do.

That being said, sports are a great bonding experience. Either watching sports or participating in them offers you as a father to take part in something your son loves. There are several ways you can bond with your son in sports.

- Coach your son in whatever sport he is in

- Watch your son play in his sport from the stands and cheer him on

- Help your son practice his favorite sport

- Watch sports on television with your son and talk about your favorite teams

- Play backyard games of football, baseball, and soccer. Often, this will be what your son enjoys the most because there is no pressure, just fun with Dad.

When you participate in sports or activities with your son, you begin to learn a lot about him. Many fathers and sons talk about things in their lives over a game of catch. Sometimes sports are the best things that fathers and sons can relate to.

OUTLETS FOR ENERGY

As was previously discussed, boys have an abundance of energy, and many places can serve as an outlet for that energy.

Sports

Sports have been mentioned several times in this chapter, and that is because it is a great outlet for boys' energy, as well as something they enjoy. As a father, you should encourage your son to get involved in sports, but do not pressure him. You do not want to become a dad who insists that your son be a star. He may not be a star, but as long as he works hard with the team, that should be enough. There are several types of sports your son can participate in, each with its own benefits.

- Team sports: These are sports where your son competes with a team and is a working part of an athletic machine. He comes to rely on his teammates and vice versa. Team sports teach your son about teamwork and cooperation to achieve a goal. Some team sports that may interest your son include basketball, soccer, baseball, football, and hockey.

- Solo sports: These are sports where your son competes against other individuals. This teaches your son to rely on himself and to be an individual, while also teaching him to try hard to achieve a goal by himself. Some solo sports that may interest your son include golf, track and field, and swimming.

- Solo team sport: These are sports where your son competes individually on a team against others. It is a hybrid of team and solo sports, and it has the benefits of both. Some solo team sports that your son may be interested in include wrestling, golf, tennis, and gymnastics.

Of course, your son does not have to participate in sports. There are other athletic endeavours he can try. Dancing is something that may interest your son, and it comes in many forms, including ballet, jazz, tap, and hip-hop. Dancing is not the sole domain of girls anymore. It can often be harder to do than most sports, and is also physically demanding.

When your son gets involved in sports, you need to help him understand the messages he may get while playing. While you may tell your son that he should respect others, he may have trouble understanding why you are telling him to body check the opposing hockey players into the boards and show no mercy to the other team. First, you should watch how you act at sporting events. It can be hard not to get excited, but that can embarrass your son. Tell your son that he can take the same things you have taught him about how to treat others, and use that when he is playing sports. This is where sportsmanship comes into play, and it is one of the most important things you can teach your son.

You should be the role model for your son when he is playing sports. Do not yell, scream, or argue with the coach or officials. Be courteous to other people in the bleachers, and you will find that your son will begin to mirror that behavior. As the father, it is important for you to set sportsmanship rules to show what is allowed and what is not. If you feel your son is not playing in a sportsmanlike way, you can talk to him and tell him that if he does not change his sportsmanship, he will not be playing. Sportsmanship is such an important thing to teach children that sometimes strict rules need to be in place.

When you are watching televised sports with your son and you see someone showing off or making fun of other players, explain to your son that is not what real athletes do. Tell him that it is okay to celebrate when you win, but while it is easy to be a sore loser, it is just as easy to be a sore winner. Tell him he should never rub the success of a sporting event in the face of an opponent. This will simply motivate the opponent to beat him in the next game. Tell your son that the following behavior has no place in sports, and if he displays this behavior he will not be playing anymore:

- Cheating: This is not sportsmanlike. This is especially important in the steroid era of some sports, where the player your son idolizes could be taking steroids.

- Criticizing others: If you see your son criticizing his teammates, coaches, the other team, or the officials, you should put a stop to it immediately. Tell him that the real leaders of the team are those who motivate, not criticize.

- Losing temper: It is natural to be mad when something does not go your way in sports, but show your son that losing his temper is not acceptable. In this case, you can lead by example. When you are watching sports on television and a bad play costs the game, do not get mad and yell at the players. This teaches your son that when something does not go his way, he should yell and scream.

- Blaming others: Your son may blame others on the team if something does not go right. This is unacceptable behavior because it will cause the other players to dislike your son and not want to play with him. Teach your son that when he loses a game, he should look at how he played and assess if there are ways to improve. He can work on his own techniques, as well as on being a good leader. Instead of blaming others on the team, he should talk with them and help them become better players.

- Arguing with officials: When you are watching baseball and the coach screams at the umpire, do not say, "That's right, you tell him! That was a horrible call!" You are teaching your son that it is okay to yell at officials. The officials are often volunteers, and it shows a complete lack of respect when your son is yelling at them. It is tough when things do not go right in sports, but arguing with the officials will only get the officials watching more closely and waiting for a mistake.

Reward and encourage good behavior with sportsmanship.

- Congratulate others: Teach your son that when someone else succeeds on the field, it is important to congratulate him or her. Being jealous does not help the team, but showing your teammates you are happy for their success does help.

- Be a good loser: No one likes to lose, but when your son loses, he needs to show appreciation for a good game. Tell him that even if others on your team do not, he should lead by example and shake not only the hands of the opposing team, but also the hands of the officials. This will earn him respect and will probably get others to do the same, making him a leader on the team.

- Never hurt anyone: Teach your son that he should never intend to hurt anyone. If someone is hurt, the real leader on the team helps the opposing player. Tell your son stories about real-life athletes who selflessly helped others, even opponents.

Sportsmanship is something that can stay with your son through his life. The examples you set will be what teaches him to be a good person and a good player with his team and in his sport.

Video game systems

Video games are an excellent outlet for energy. With the Nintendo Wii, the world of video games has changed. Now, kids can actually burn off energy by playing video games, while improving their reflexes and hand-eye coordination. Whether it is acting out the motions of Wii Sports or Wii Sports Resort, being a rock star with Guitar Hero, or getting in shape with Wii Fit, there are many options available to your son to use his energy in a video game system. This is especially beneficial on rainy days or during the winter when it may be too cold outside. Your son can play the video games, burn off energy, and stay in shape.

Now, it is important to note that while your son can play video games to burn off energy, video games should not be the only things on which you rely. He needs to go outdoors to stay healthy. He will not get outdoor benefits if he stays indoors. Balance video game time with outdoor time to teach your son that while video games are fun, it is important to socialize outside and enjoy what nature provides. When you play outside with your son, you are also bonding with him. You can play video games with your son, but do not let that be the only thing that bonds the two of you.

It is also important that you have guidelines for video game playing. All modern video games come with a rating system, and depending on the age of your child, some games will be appropriate while others will not. Here is the rating system and what each rating means:

- eC: These games are meant for children in early childhood, between the ages of two and 10. Typically, these games will be based on childhood television shows.

- E: This is a game recommended for all ages. These games contain minimal violence of any kind. Examples of this type of game include the Mario series.

- E10+: This is a game that is suitable for children older than 10 years of age. There is sometimes mild violence, blood, and profanity. Examples of this include Banjo-Kazooie, Lego Star Wars, and TMNT.

- T: This rating means that the game is meant for teens between the ages of 13 and 17. These games may contain crude humor, moderate language, suggestive themes, and violence. Call of Duty and the Guitar Hero series are examples of this.

- M: These games are for gamers older than 17. These games contain blood and gore, sexual themes and content, drugs and alcohol, and intense violence. Examples of this include the Halo series and Fallout 3.

- AO: This rating means the game is only meant for adults (18+). These games feature sex, nudity, violence, blood, and gore. Only 25 games have had this rating since 1994, including Grand Theft Auto.

COMMUNICATING WITH YOUR SON

In the past, there was an unwritten rule that fathers and sons did not talk about what they were feeling. Thankfully, these days seem to be disappearing, and talking with your children about what you are both feeling is becoming more acceptable and normal. There are two extremes with communication. There is the "non-communication father" who avoids too much talking, and there is the father who requires communication, even when there is nothing to communicate about.

As a father, you should look to be in the middle. You should communicate, but if your children have nothing to talk about, do not make them start talking. For example, when your son comes home from school and you ask, "How did your day go?" listen to what he has to say. You will learn a lot about your son based on what he tells you about school. When and where you talk to your son is also important. If you stop your son in the hallway on his way out, you probably will not get a long conversation. Therefore, you should try and find times to talk to your son. Have your son help you with dinner, go outside and play catch, or sit at the table with something to drink and talk about whatever is going on in both your lives.

Talking to a teenage son

Having a talk with your 8-year-old son is a cakewalk compared to talking to a teenage son sometimes. As a result of puberty, your son may not want to talk with you, choosing instead to be alone. However, it is important you talk to your son through this confusing time to help make things easier on him and yourself. There are many ways you can talk to your teenage son, but follow these steps for successful communication.

1. Take your son somewhere that has no distractions, such as video games or television. Take him to the park or to his favorite restaurant.

2. Rather than talking about the things that interest you, talk about things that interest him, or things that interest both of you.

3. Sometimes it can be easier to talk when another person reveals something about him or herself. Tell your son stories about when you were a teenager. This will help him relate to and communicate with you. Make sure you talk about the differences you see between what teens went through when you were young, and what teens are currently going through.

4. One of the most difficult things for a teenage boy to talk about is relationships, both with friends and in dating. Tell your son about the relationships you had during

your teenage years, letting him know both the good and the bad.

5. If your son comes to you and asks for advice, give it to him. Also, give him some relatable examples from your own life that can help answer his question.

6. It can be hard to share feelings, so tell your son that you appreciate when he talks about the events, information, and emotions in his life.

BEING A GOOD ROLE MODEL

A father is the template that a son uses to determine who he is going to be when he grows up. You are your son's role model, and what you do will influence your son's personality for the rest of his life. You need to set a positive example for your son. There are several things you need to do to be a good role model.

1. When you make promises, especially promises to your son, keep them. Teach your son that his word is one of the most important things he has, and he should never break it. If you tell him this, and then forget to pick him up from soccer practice, it sends the wrong message.

2. Show that honesty and ethics are important. Always tell the truth — if he finds out you lied, it will shatter any belief in honesty. You are the one your son trusts the most.

3. Treat others with respect to show your son how to treat people. Some people feel that those who work as servers in restaurants are fair game for insults. If the waitress gets your order wrong and you yell at her, you are show-ing your son that it is all right to yell at others when

something does not go your way. Not only do you look like a jerk to everyone else, you are sending the wrong message to your son. A good way to think is to act the way you want other people to act around you. Treat people how you want to be treated and your son will follow that example.

4.   Refrain from foul language around your son. If you are swearing with every third word, you will only teach your son colorful words that he may end up using in school. If you find that you cannot watch your language, get a "swear jar." Whenever you swear, put money in the jar. You will not only curb the bad language, but you will also have a good amount of money that you can use to buy something for the family.

5.   How you dress says a lot, and it serves as an example for your son. If you dress well, you are teaching your children to dress well. If you dress poorly, your children will match that. You also want to set an example for your son by showing him that you can look good without buying brand new, trendy clothes that are too expensive.

6.   You want your son to eat healthy, but you set the wrong example if you eat fast food. Take your son on walks, participate in physical activity, and eat healthy — you will find that your son will do the same.

7.   Being a part of the community is important, and you can show that to your son by being involved in activities around the community. By helping and respecting the community, you teach your son to learn by example. It is also a great way to show your son how to socialize with

others, as well as the importance of being helpful to those around you.

DATING

As your son gets older, he is going to start thinking about dating. When he does, it is up to you to talk to him about it. There is no right answer for when your son should start dating, so that is generally up to you. Some parents are fine with their children dating at age 13, but others want their children to wait until they are at least 16. As the father, whatever you think is best should be what you go with. However, you should remember that teenage boys are going to want to date, and giving them the opportunity gives you the chance to talk to them about it.

Remember that communication is very important with your son. You should be available to talk if he has questions. Tell him you are there for him if he needs to talk, tell him you love him, and explain that if he has dating questions, you can answer them. If he is younger and confused by the feelings, tell him that it is natural for him to feel the way he does, and that he should not be embarrassed.

Explain to your son that on the date, he needs to be respectful to the girl and treat her properly. If your son does not learn how to treat a girl properly, he may find that he spends several lonely years before figuring out how to act. He could also end up getting in trouble with the law or the girl's father if he does not treat the girl properly. Tell him what is appropriate and inappropriate to do. You should also stress to your son that while his hormones may be raging, when a girl says "no," he must respect that. You should make sure that your son knows that his date deserves his respect, and should be treated in a courteous manner.

Your son has probably learned a great deal about sex through friends and sex education classes in school, but it is important that you talk to your son about sex before he begins dating. It can be awkward to talk about, but it is essential that you do. Explain to him that his friends will pressure him to have sex when dating, but he should not give in to the pressure until both he and his girlfriend are ready.

Providing your son with information about sexually transmitted diseases is also important. Most health departments will have plenty of informational pamphlets, but you can also go online to find information. Tell your son about the dangers of sexually transmitted diseases and unplanned pregnancy, and why it is important to practice safe sex, or even celibacy.

When your son begins dating, ask him to bring the girl home for you to meet. You should meet the girl who has infatuated your son, and she should meet you and the rest of the family. Talk with your son's date and learn about her because you want to be comfortable with the idea of your son dating her. When you ask your son to bring his date over for dinner, explain that you are not trying to interfere, you just want to meet the girl he is spending so much time with.

CONCLUSION

Raising a son when you are a single father is not always easy. You may want to give up and pack it all in sometimes, but it is important that you do not. Your son looks up to you, even during the troubling teenager years. Your son sees you as a role model and as the person he wants to be when he grows up. If you have younger children, you are a superhero to them. You can do no wrong and are always there to save the day.

As a father, you need to help your son through his childhood and teen years. Provide him with an outlet for his energy, and show him how to act around others. Answer his questions about puberty, talk with him, and learn about what may be troubling him. You can have an amazing relationship with your son as a single father, and it all begins by showing an interest in and spending time with your son.

12 | Dealing With A Daughter

> *"A truly rich man is one whose children run into his arms when his hands are empty."*
>
> — Anonymous

Being a single dad to a son is generally thought to be easier than being a single dad to a daughter. You can at least relate to a son because you went through the same issues during childhood and puberty. With a daughter, it can be a completely unknown world, but that does not mean it is one you should stay away from. Being the single dad of a daughter is a wonderful experience that few single fathers would trade for the world. As a single dad, you will learn about your daughter, which can make you a richer person.

When you first become a single father to a daughter, there will be a range of emotions your daughter will be going through. In this early stage, it may be hard to connect with your daughter. If you have gone through a divorce, there will be some distance between you and your daughter. If your daughter has lost her mother due to death, she will likely want to be very close with you.

HELP IS ALWAYS APPRECIATED

When you are a new single father of a daughter, you may want to look at getting female help. It is important for a single father to ensure there is some sort of female mentor in his daughter's life if her mother is deceased. There are several people who will fit this criteria, including:

- One of your daughter's grandmothers
- One of her aunts
- Your female friends
- The mother of one of your daughter's friends

It is important that you find someone who can serve as a strong and capable role model for your daughter. This does not mean you cannot be a role model. You are the first man in your daughter's life, and that means you have a huge influence on her and the type of person she becomes.

DO NOT OVERPROTECT

There is a tendency for single fathers to over-protect their daughters. All fathers want to be the knight in shining armor who rescues his daughter whenever the time comes. Being too overprotective of your daughter may seem cute at first, but as time goes on, it can begin to have a negative impact. If you always "rescue" your daughter and dictate what she can and cannot do because you are afraid she may get hurt, she will either rebel or become overly-dependent on you. Both of these are outcomes you want to avoid. While it may be hard, you should ensure that your daughter has to struggle with some of life's problems and challenges herself, no different than you would with your son. Limited risks are all right because they will help your daughter build confidence in herself, which is important for her success later in life.

WHAT TO EXPECT

If you have gone through a divorce, you can expect your daughter to recover more quickly than your son. Divorce researchers Judith Wallerstein and Joan Kelly state that girls are able to recover quicker, but they suffer from what is called the "sleeper effect," which means the effects of the separation between you and your wife will not show up until adolescence or later.

As stated above, after a daughter will usually become attached to her father after she loses her mother. Your daughter will feel secure knowing that she will always have you, and that will create a strong bond between the two of you. She will feel comforted and supported by your love, and will feel confident in it. If you lose your wife through death, it is important to talk with your daughter and have her express what she is feeling. Talking is one of the best ways to deal with grief, especially for daughters.

More time with daughter

Whether you have gone through a divorce, or lost your wife due to death, you will find that you are spending a lot more time with your daughter than you did before. This means there are some things to remember when dealing with your daughter versus your son.

First and foremost, always give your full attention to your daughter. If she is talking to you, do not listen out of the corner of your ear while you watch television or work on the computer. This is important because if you do not show an interest when your daughter talks to you, she is going to sense it and eventually stop talking to you. This is especially important for a daughter. On average, girls are more apt to talk about what they are feeling and look for support through communication. This is in sharp contrast to the average boy who will become more withdrawn and shy away from communication.

Listen for the meaning behind your daughter's words. When she tells you about her day, listen to what she says — you can learn a lot. Your daughter will often talk about how she is feeling about her relationships with other people, what is bothering her, her hopes and dreams, and various other things. Listen to what she says because it will tell you what is going on behind the scenes in your daughter's life.

Privacy

The need for privacy will be important for your daughter, even before adolescence. Many fathers will often bathe the children together, or with him, during their early years (before age four, typically) and most experts feel that there is no problem with this. However, as time goes on, your daughter is going to start asking for more privacy, and not only during bath time. She will want time to herself in other circumstances, so you need to provide her with her own room and time on the computer where she does not have to worry about someone watching everything she does (parental controls can help here). Your daughter will want time to herself, so it is important to give her privacy. Be there for her when she wants to talk, but stand to the side when she is being more introspective.

DEALING WITH PUBERTY

For single fathers, puberty can be an awkward topic of conversation. Fathers often feel that they are completely out of their element during this time. However, it is important that you answer your daughter's questions and talk with her during adolescence. Having female help, no different than after a divorce or death, can come in handy, too.

Expect that between the ages of 11 and 13 (although it can be as early as nine, especially in obese children), your daughter will begin to go through puberty. Several changes will begin to take place that will continue for several years through her teenage years. If you are the single father of a daughter who has lost her mother, most of the answers are going to come through you. If you are divorced, your daughter will probably talk to her mother about these things, but that does not mean you should not know about them.

The following Web sites include information about what your daughter is going through during her teenage years. Prepare yourself by researching this information, so you will be ready if your daughter has any questions.

- U.S. Department of Health (**www.hhs.gov**): Go to this site, click the "Families" tab, then click "Teenage Health" under the "Teens" heading. Information about depression, alcohol, sexually transmitted diseases, specific female hormone issues, sexual health, the Human Papilloma Virus vaccine, and more topics are included.

- WebMD (**www.webmd.com**): This Web site has myriad pages of information about any health-related question you may have about puberty or other issues.

- Tampax (**www.tampax.com**): This Web site has information about women's health (topics such as ovulation, fertility, cramps, breast health, and yeast infections), as well as an "Ask Iris" section, where anyone can ask questions, such as, "When is the best time to talk to my daughter about sex?" There is also a section on how to insert a tampon (tell your daughter to read this section).

- Center for Young Women's Health (**www.youngwomen-shealth.org**): This Web site provides education, clinical care, research, and health care advocacy for teen girls and young women. Nutrition and fitness information, emotional guides, sexuality information, health guides, gynecology, parent guides, and "guys' guides" are all available here.

Menstruation

Generally, a girl begins to menstruate around 12 years old, depending on several factors. Some girls begin at eight or nine years of age. Your daughter's periods will be irregular for about one year, but should become more regular, arriving every 28 to 30 days. Her period will last anywhere from three to seven days.

If you are divorced, there is a chance your daughter will have her first period while she is staying with you. This is why it is important to talk to your daughter about menstruation beforehand. Most daughters will think their fathers will have no idea about what is going on. Tell her that she can tell you when she does get her period. Explain to her that it is a normal occurrence that happens in all women and will continue until she is older, when she will then go through menopause.

Tell her that she may experience cramps before each period starts. Again, if she has not gone through it before, the cramps may be worrisome for her; talking to her about it can eliminate that worry. She may feel tired, nauseous, cranky, and bloated.

If you have female friends, ask them what you should be buying for your daughter in terms of sanitary pads or tampons. If there are no female friends for you to talk to, ask a pharmacist. The pharmacist will most likely recommend sanitary pads instead of tampons for a girl who just started her period.

It is also important to tell your daughter that when she has used a pad or tampon, that she should wrap it in paper and throw it away. Tell her not to throw it into the toilet because it could cause the toilet to back up.

Training bras

As your daughter matures during puberty, her breasts are going to develop, which means you will need to buy training bras for her. If your daughter is late in developing, you may feel that training bras are not needed, but try to see it from her perspective. As your daughter's friends develop, possibly before her, she will embarrassed that she is still wearing undershirts. Therefore, as she begins to develop, you can take her to get a training bra.

Like with menstruation, many fathers will feel awkward doing this. If you do, ask a female relative or friend to do it for you. If no one can do it for you, you must take your daughter to the store to help her buy a training bra. Most department stores will have expert female fitters who can go in the dressing room with your daughter to help her find a training bra that fits properly and will be comfortable for her. She may feel strange having someone help her, but explain to her that the person helping her is a professional. After this point, take another trip to the store every six months to a year to find a bra for your daughter that will fit her changing shape.

Questions

When your daughter is going through puberty, she will have questions about her changing body and changing emotions. It is normal for fathers to feel uncomfortable around these questions, but it is imperative that you answer your daughter in a frank and clear manner. If you are stammering and seem ill at ease talking to her about what is going on, she may think there is something wrong with being curious — that is not the image you want to project.

When you answer questions without stammering and seeming uncomfortable, you are showing trust and respect to your daughter. That will help raise her self-confidence, which is incredibly important during the formative teen years.

Hair growth

Not unlike what happens with boys, your daughter will begin growing hair on her legs, underarms, and pubic area during adolescence. If you are divorced and sharing custody, your wife will probably talk about shaving legs and armpits, but if you are widowed or have full custody, it may be up to you. Again, you can have a female friend or relative talk to your daughter about it if you feel the situation is difficult for you to handle.

If you do need to talk to your daughter about shaving her armpits and legs, you can simply explain that as the hair grows, she may want to shave her legs and armpits. You can easily show her how by letting her watch you shave your face, or if you want to go the whole nine yards, you can shave your own legs to show how it is done.

Emotions

During puberty, your daughter may feel embarrassed, uncomfortable, or even fat in her changing body. Chances are, she is comparing her rate of development with other girls she knows. If she starts late, she may wonder why the other girls are changing and she is not. If she starts early with puberty, she may wonder why the other girls are not changing, and she will have to deal with increased attention from boys.

This is where you come in. Talk to her and tell her that what she is feeling is normal. Explain that she will catch up with the other girls, or that the other girls will catch up with her. It is important that you tell her she should not be embarrassed, that she is not fat, and that everything happening will pass within a few years.

CREATING A BOND

It is imperative that you create a bond with your daughter from an early age. A father-daughter bond can be incredibly strong and remain that way for the rest of your life. If you have gone through a divorce, you will want to bond with your daughter out of fear of losing her like you lost your wife. If you are widowed, bonding with your daughter provides a link to your deceased wife.

Do things she likes

There is a tendency among single fathers to try to get daughters to like things that usually appeal to boys. While there is nothing wrong with this, you should not forget about spending quality time with her doing things she likes. If you have a young daughter who likes tea parties, then you better put on your best tea party hat because spending time with her in those situations creates a strong bond. As your daughter grows older, she is going to have different interests, ones you should share with her. If she wants to ride horses, find a way to make it happen and participate. If she wants to play baseball, go to the games and help out with the team. Try to choose activities that you are both going to enjoy together. When you spend quality time together, you strengthen your connection.

Acceptance and affection

We all want to feel accepted and loved, so make sure your daughter feels as though she is loved and accepted by you. Instead of being judgemental of her, support and encourage her. When she does well, praise her; when she fails at something, help her succeed next time. Affection is important because your daughter needs to know that you care about her. While you may have trouble expressing emotions to your daughter, a simple hug or saying "I love you" can go a long way in making your daughter feel as though she is loved and appreciated by her father.

Get involved

Just as you take part in activities she likes, you should get involved in your daughter's life. By doing so, you create a strong bond and can watch to see what is going on with her mind and emotions, especially during puberty. Some ways to get involved in your daughter's life include:

1. Attend parent-teacher conferences.

2. Learn who her friends are, where she spends her time, and what some of her goals are. You can do this by simply talking to her.

3. Do a school project together or work together on something for the house. If you are building something in the house, ask if your daughter would like to help you.

4. If your daughter wants to volunteer, participate with her. Volunteering together gives you a close connection, and it helps you learn more about her as you talk with her.

RAISED BY A SINGLE FATHER

Leslie Truex
Raised by a single father

I was very young when I went to live with my dad, and I did not know anything different. It was quite normal for me. I can say that I have fond memories, and as a parent myself now, I have a better appreciation of his parenting. He was very attentive. We played games and watched television together. He cooked dinner for me and taught me how to make lunch to pack to school. Looking back, I can see there were some unconventional aspects. My father was young, so he drove an MG (British sports car) with his kid standing in the front seat (we did not know about seat belts then). I grew up listening to rock music. I went to a preschool for day care. Most kids left at lunch, which now I realize were kids who had at-home moms. My father had to work Saturday nights, so I had a baby-sitter those nights. In that respect it was different, as nearly everyone else I knew did not have full-day preschool or baby-sitters.

On a daily basis, I did not feel different. But, there were times when people were curious. Since it was unusual to be raised by a man during that time, many people assumed my mother was dead or crazy (she was neither). My father tells a story about when he signed me up for kindergarten, and the principal said that I did not look like a child from a broken home — I was a very outgoing, social child. My father was offended by this. He did not feel our home was broken and did not like that expectations would be different for me because I was in a single-parent home.

I was an only child, so it was just my dad and I, and we had lots of fun. I love Disneyland, and he would make the eight-hour drive with me fairly often. He would put me in the back of his MG at night and I would wake up the next morning in Disneyland. We have a lot of "special" memories that I am not sure kids from other families have. For example, if you were to ask him about a favorite song of ours, I know he would say the 52nd Street Bridge song. We boo-hooed over the movie Born Free. He brought my big swing set home in a box in the back of his MG. It was quite a sight.

One Christmas, when I woke him at 4 a.m. to open presents, he got up instead of sending me back to bed. So, I guess some of the best parts were that it was just us two, and I did not have to share him with siblings.

My dad will say sometimes that we raised each other. He later remarried when I was a teen, and had more children. Their experience is different than mine. I think they are close to him, but it is different.

MAKEUP AND CLOTHING

For many fathers, the first sign that their daughters are no longer little girls anymore is when makeup comes into the picture. If you and your ex-wife share custody of your daughter, you both need to talk about makeup and when you will allow her to wear it. If your wife says 12 is a good age, but you think 16 is best, you will have to compromise. Remember, consistency is important; this is not a battle between you and your ex-wife.

In regards to clothing, your daughter may feel the need to wear provocative clothing. On the one hand, this means your daughter is happy with her body and wants to show it off. On the other hand, it may not be appropriate. A simple dress code can be enforced. This can include no exposed midriff when out for dinner, visiting family, or going to church. However, do not restrict your daughter too much or the natural desire to rebel will come forward. Let her find her own style, with you offering fatherly suggestions along the way.

Rather than rejecting what she is wearing, you should talk to your daughter and work out a solution. Try the following:

1.   When the stress level is low and your daughter is relaxed, ask to talk to her about clothing.

2.   Start by complimenting your daughter: say that she has several nice clothes, or that her hair looks good. Make sure that the compliment focuses on a decision she has made. In relation to clothing, this means saying that the shirt she bought herself looks great. If you only compliment what you bought her, you will get nowhere.

3.   Do not attack all of her clothes, which will be the same as attacking her sense of style. Instead, mention some of the clothing, or just an article of clothing, that you do not care for. Explain to her your feelings, rather than saying something hurtful like, "No daughter of mine will wear a shirt that makes her look like that." Say something like, "You are a wonderful person and I do not want people making snap judgments about you based on how you dress."

4.   Listen to your daughter's reasons for wearing the things that you may not like. She may say you are old-fashioned, or that all the kids are dressing like she is. Explain to her that she can either dress like everyone, or she can be an

individual and find her own style. Explain that there is nothing wrong with being current with style, but sometimes that style crosses the line.

5.   Instead of vetoing her clothes, reach a compromise. Many teenagers just want to be treated like adults, and reaching a compromise is a good way to do that. If you do not like a low-cut shirt she wears, give the option that if she agrees to not wear the shirt to school, you will let the issue over the skirt slide for now.

6.   After the conversation, let your daughter know that you care about her and that you only want the best for her. Tell her that you are there to talk to at any point.

DATING

For many fathers, dating is a four-letter word when it comes to daughters. However, your daughter will date and instead of hoping she does not, simply talk to her about dating and, by extension, sex. The main concern for fathers is their daughters' safety.

When your daughter starts to date, talk to her before you start flying off the handle at the prospect of your daughter going out with boys. Tell your daughter that it is important to understand that some boys only want one thing — sex. Explain that she should not feel pressured to do anything, no matter what her friends or boyfriend say. Tell her that you love her no matter what and you want her to be safe. By talking to her as adult, you will get her to listen to what you are saying much easier than if you tell her that she cannot date until you say she can.

Try some of the following tips to help ensure you have more peace of mind when your daughter begins to date.

1. Implement a curfew. This is to ensure that the boy brings your daughter home on time. If your daughter comes home late, unless she has a good excuse, you should reprimand her.

2. Provide your daughter with a cell phone. With a cell phone, your daughter can call and tell you if she will be late. Make sure the cell phone battery is charged before she goes out.

3. It is important that you not only meet the boy your daughter is dating, but that you get his cell phone number, as well. When a boy comes to the door to pick up your daughter, it shows respect. If he are willing to face you, it shows a bit of bravery, too. Tell your daughter that you just want to meet her boyfriend, but you will not embarrass her or threaten the boy, which is a legitimate worry for a daughter. Shake the hand of the boy dating your daughter and explain when you would like your daughter home.

4. Even though you have your daughter's cell phone number, you do not need to call her during the date. Calling her too much is unnecessary and your daughter will feel as though she is being controlled and watched. Tell her that the only reason you would call her on the date is if it was important, otherwise she may choose not to pick up.

5. When your daughter goes out on a date, ask her where they will go. This is not an invasion of privacy — it is just

so you know where she will be. If there is a change of plans, ask her to call you to let you know. You do not need to know what she is doing and every detail about her date, just the basics.

If your daughter's boyfriend breaks up with her, or vice versa, respect her feelings. She may say that she has lost her true love, and although you know that is probably not the case, support and comfort her. Do not just tell your daughter that she will find someone else and teenage romance is not something to cry over. Tell her that you understand it hurts right now, and give examples and experiences from your own life so she can see that you went through the same thing. Try to distract her with things the two of you like to do together, but do not buy her presents in the hopes she will stop crying. That being said, if she wants to cry it out in her room and be alone, let her do that. She will feel better in time and life will go on. Just make sure she knows that you are there to talk if she needs to.

Talking about sex

The topic of sex is on the list of uncomfortable things for fathers to talk to their daughters about. If your daughter is roughly 15 or older, there is a chance she may be having sex. According to the National Center for Health Statistics (NCHS), half of all teens have had sex by the age of 16. It is essential to talk to your daughter about sex because the United States has the highest rate of teen pregnancy in the developed world. Currently, South Korea has the lowest teen pregnancy rate of three out of every 1,000. The United States, in contrast, has a teen pregnancy rate of 53 out of every 1,000. Every year, three million teens get sexually transmitted diseases, according to the NCHS.

Tell your daughter that if she is having sex, you want to make sure she is safe. Talk to her about the dangers of STDs, AIDS, and pregnancy, and how condoms can potentially prevent all of that. If your daughter wants to start taking birth control pills, do not refuse. Instead, let her talk to her doctor about birth control pills, what they do, and get a prescription for them. You should be open to the idea of birth control for your daughter after the age of 13. This is not only because of teen pregnancy, but birth control also help to regulate a girl's menstruation.

Tell her that she does not have to give in to peer pressure — if a boy tells her that he will not like her if she does not have sex, he is a boy she should dump. Your daughter needs to know that no matter what happens, you will love her. By showing her that respect and being up front with her about topics like sex, you are treating her like an adult, which will help her act like an adult.

HPV vaccine

One topic you should approach with your daughter is whether or not she wants to get the Human Papilloma Virus vaccine. This vaccine will greatly minimize the chances of your daughter getting cervical cancer after she has become sexually active. The vaccine prevents certain types of HPV.

If you share custody with your ex-wife, then you should talk to her about whether you want to get the HPV vaccine for your daughter. It is also important to note that the vaccine is not 100 percent effective in preventing cervical cancer, but it will greatly lower the chances. If cervical cancer has been a problem in either your ex-wife's or your family history, you should get the vaccine for your daughter.

BEING A POSITIVE ROLE MODEL

Your daughter looks up to you from a young age, and the way you act says a lot about how your daughter will act later in life. By being a positive role model, you can teach your daughter about being a good person, and how to act throughout life. There are several things you can do to help ensure you are a good role model.

- If you were raised in a home where there was a clear distinction between men and women and their roles in the home, get rid of those archaic beliefs. Your daughter is not in the home to be the lady of the house. By thinking that men work and women stay home, you are not being a positive role model. You should break free of this habit and show your daughter that men can keep things in order in the home, while women can achieve anything they want. If you are saying things that are offensive about women in the home, you are setting a bad example for both your daughter and your son, if you have one.

- Actions speak louder than words, so let your daughter see you working around the house, cooking, and cleaning.

- Help shatter stereotypes with your daughter by getting her help with tasks that were previously associated with men, like fixing the car.

- Be kind to other people so your daughter can see how to treat others.

- Do not make inappropriate comments about others, especially other women, in front of your daughter.

- Show respect to others and to your daughter.

- Have a positive attitude when working through problems. Your daughter will see this and respond to it.

- Celebrate when you achieve your goals and always try to better yourself. This is one of the best things you can do as a role model because it will set a good example for your daughter.

CONCLUSION

As the single father of a daughter, you may feel the need to be overprotective. You may want to protect her from anything bad that could happen. While this is noble, it is not the best course of action. Your daughter needs to think for herself and act independently as she grows into womanhood. She needs to find her own path and achieve her own goals. She needs to know that she can achieve what she wants. As her father, you can show her that.

As a father, you should talk to your daughter and learn more about her. You need to learn what it is to be a female so that you can help relate to her. Answering her questions when she is going through puberty, consoling her when she breaks up with a boy, and congratulating her on her achievements are all ways to raise a great daughter.

Although fathers may be able to relate to sons easier, they often have an incredibly strong bond with their daughters. As a father, you are a major role model for your daughter and the first man in her life. There is a great deal of responsibility, and you can help your daughter progress from a girl to a young woman.

> *"There are three stages of a man's life: He believes in Santa Claus, he doesn't believe in Santa Claus, he is Santa Claus."*
>
> — Anonymous

Time heals all wounds, and whether you went through a divorce or widowhood, you are eventually going to move on and possibly find love again. When that happens, you need to deal with the issues that come up with dating as a single father. How are your children going to react? Will you find someone who wants to possibly assume the role of the mother?

These are all questions that will go through your head. Possibly the most important question you will ask yourself will be, "Can I be happy again?" You can, and you will be surprised at how your children react when they learn that someone else is filling your heart after an extended period of being a bachelor.

WHEN SHOULD YOU START DATING AGAIN?

You will have friends who tell you that you should jump back into dating right away, and you will have family members who tell you to take it slow. To whom should you listen? The simple answer is neither. The only person you should listen to is yourself — you will know when you are ready to get back into the dating game.

You probably will not want to start dating too soon after you lost your wife due to death. If you were divorced, you will want to wait and assess what went wrong so you do not make the same mistakes, or you will want to jump right into the dating world to get your confidence back. You should ask yourself if you are ready to get back into dating, and consider your reasons for dating again. Are you dating because you are lonely, or are you dating to get confidence? Do you want to date so you can show your ex-wife you bounced back quicker than she did, or are you hoping that you may find love?

It is important to remember that while you may try to get into the dating scene, sometimes a relationship just simply happens. Perhaps you are at the grocery store and you meet a nice woman you end up dating. Another possibility is that you start dating the single mother of one of your child's friends. These are unexpected, but when these situations happen, seize the opportunity if it makes you happy. If you want to get into the dating scene with more control, start looking for singles.

Places to look for singles

The first place you can look for singles is on the social scene. This can include networking groups, social groups, and the bar and restaurant scenes. While most people try these places in an effort to meet someone, it can be hard to strike up a long-term relationship in this scenarios. If you are nervous about being in groups or going to the bar by yourself, go with some single friends. When you are with friends, it is often easier to talk to women and feel more at ease.

The second place you can look is on the Internet, which is becoming popular with single dads. The great thing about the Internet is you can go to dating sites and find someone who matches what you are looking for almost exactly. If you are looking for someone who does not mind dating a guy with kids, there are Web sites for that. Some of the more popular sites you can check out if you are looking for a relationship are:

- Match.com (**www.match.com**) — $29.99/month

- eHarmony.com (**www.eharmony.com**) — $19.95-$59.96/month

- AmericanSingles.com (**www.americansingles.com**) — $7.94/month

- SingleParentMatch.com (**www.singleparentmatch.com**) — $29.95/month

When you are using a dating site, it is easy to create a profile — just sign up for the service. Pick a photo of yourself that you think is flattering and shows off your best qualities, but make it a tasteful photo. Include what you are looking for in a partner and write about yourself. Remember to be honest. There is no sense lying about yourself in the hopes it will bring someone to you.

WHEN DADS DATE AGAIN

Irene Lacota
President,
It's Just Lunch International
www.itsjustlunch.com

CLASSIFIED CASE STUDIES

directly from the experts

It can indeed be hard for dads to start dating again: They are busy with their kids and careers, and do not have a lot of time to meet people. Some of them are also facing issues of child care when they want to go on a dates (same as single moms), and they also want to spend more time with kids. Much depends on the custody situation fathers have with their ex-spouses. Another factor, certainly, is the age of the child. Children younger than 10 can make dating very hard due to emotional strains and child care options. Many of our single dads like us to arrange dates when their children are with their moms. Another factor that can make dating hard for men is that they are more vulnerable than some people might think — or more than men might admit. We recognize that at It's Just Lunch, and try to advise and encourage them accordingly.

One successful couple that we set up both had children who were very important to them, and were looking to date other single parents. Their children were a huge bond for them so they ended up going on several dates, including family-oriented events with the kids. However, we have learned from our single-father clients that they are not necessarily looking for someone to be a mother to their children. Instead, they are looking for someone to be with. That has been another definite factor in successful matches.

Our members have described a few road blocks to us. Time seems to be the biggest obstacle — that is, having time to meet new people, and meeting the right type of people who will understand and be accepting of their children.

Another challenge for fathers is finding women who are comfortable dating a man whose ex-wife is a big part of his life because of the kids, and it is also a challenge to make sure the new girlfriend gets along with and accepts the children.

Many of the single fathers don't get to see their kids often, as more moms have primary custody, so the dads seem to want to date when they do not have their kids. One interesting thing we have also noticed is that some men, even those with children themselves, are hesitant to date women who have children younger than their own children. It is as if they are scared to have to do a "do over."

In a nutshell, it can be hard to get back into the dating game for single fathers because some of them have given up out of frustration. But, we have many single fathers who are excited for us to do all the work — we set up the dates and make reservations. Single fathers should realize that life does not end after widowhood or divorce. There are other great women out there, and It's Just Lunch can help you meet them!

TALKING TO YOUR EX-WIFE

If you divorced, you are going to have to talk to your ex-wife about the fact that you are dating, and that there are new rules as a result. Even if you do not have a good relationship with your ex-wife, you should to talk to her. First, tell your ex-wife that while you are out with your date, you do not want to get calls from her asking what you are doing or trying to pry into your business. This may not happen, but your date does not want someone who still deals with an ex-wife from afar. Your new partner may see any communication with your ex-wife as a threat.

Also, talk with your ex-wife and explain that when you have a weekend with your date, your ex cannot show up with the kids saying she has plans and needs you to watch them. You may love spending time with your kids, but you need your time for yourself. When you tell your ex-wife, let her know there is another person in your life. You do not need to tell her about the person, or how she compares with your ex-spouse. Instead, explain that you have met someone nice whom you enjoy spending time with. Be courteous and explain to your ex-wife that the children are Number One in your life, and that no relationship will interfere with your children. It is important you tell your ex-wife this because she may think that a new relationship will interfere with your commitments as a father. Assuring her that this is not the case can make the difficult conversation of a new love an easier one.

INTRODUCING THE KIDS TO YOUR DATE

When you decide to make the big step and tell your children about your new girlfriend and introduce the two of them, use the tips below. There is no right time to introduce the two parts of your life, just like there is no right time to start dating. However, when you are comfortable enough with your date and your date is comfortable enough with you, it may be the right time. Make sure that you have been dating for a while and there is a good possibility of a long-term relationship. You do not want to be introducing your children to a new woman every few weeks.

- Rather than introduce the children too soon, wait a while before making the introductions. If you are a widower, you may have to wait longer than if you are a divorcee.

- Instead of having a long weekend with everyone together for the first time, you should schedule just a few hours for the children to meet your new girlfriend. This will allow time for everyone to ease into the concept of a changing relationship and family structure.

- Do not just have your date show up to meet the children. Tell your children that you are bringing over your new girlfriend and you would like them to meet her. Preparing your children is extremely important.

- Talk to your girlfriend and tell her about your kids and their habits. If your son likes to use sarcasm as a way of breaking the ice, it would be a good idea to tell your date so she does not get offended.

- Until your children are accustomed to the concept of you with a new girlfriend, you should hold off on displaying too much affection in front of the children. Kissing and hugging may have to wait until the kids are more at ease with your new girlfriend.

- Do not expect everyone to get along right away, and do not have high expectations. If you do, it may result in things going poorly because you assumed everyone would get along.

WHAT TO AVOID WITH YOUR DATES

Your date likes you, but she does not want to hear you talk about all the things that went wrong with your previous relationship, why your marriage fell apart, or how you wish that your wife was still alive. While your date will understand that it can be hard to get past a divorce or death, she will hope that she can help you get past those problems and on to a better life with her.

- If you talk about your deceased wife too much, your girlfriend might be intimidated. Missing your deceased wife is normal; making her out to be a saint in front of your girlfriend is not.

- If you talk about how good things are between you and your ex-wife now, after the divorce, your girlfriend is going to think there is a chance you and your ex-wife may get back together. If she is hoping for a long-term relationship, she may decide it is not worth the time to invest in you if you are just going to leave her for your ex-wife.

- If you talk about how heinous you feel your ex-wife is, your date will listen and most likely side with you because she cares about you. However, creating a relationship that is built on the hate of another is a relationship that will not last.

This does not mean you should not tell your date that you are widowed or divorced. In fact, you should tell her because honesty is important. If you hide the fact you are a widower or are divorced, it may cause problems down the road when your girlfriend finds out.

WHAT YOU ARE FEELING

When you start dating, there are several feelings that you will go through. These feelings are normal, and are all part of the rebuilding process for yourself and your self-confidence.

1. You will be happy and you will feel relief. You are happy that you found someone, and you are relieved that the possibility of you living life alone just got smaller.

2. You will also be wary and feel vulnerable. The reason for this is that you lost your wife through divorce or widowhood, and you do not want to go through that again. You will be wary, but hopeful that the relationship will succeed. However, in the back of your mind you will continue to hear, "What if it fails?"

3. If you lost your wife through death, you will feel guilty. You will think you are dishonoring your deceased wife by dating someone else. The best way to look at this is to think what your wife would be thinking at that moment. Most likely, she would want you to be happy.

4. You may overcompensate in your new relationship. If you are divorced, you may feel as though you have to be more open, more loving, and happier to keep from being hurt again. While this may seem like a good idea, your girlfriend may find it suffocating.

WHAT TO TELL YOUR CHILDREN

After you have introduced your girlfriend to your children, you should talk with them about several topics:

1. Tell your children that you love them and always will. Just because there is a new woman in your life does not mean you will pay any less attention to them.

2. It is important to tell your children that you are not trying to replace their mother. They will not want their mother replaced, and if they think it will happen, they will have a rocky relationship with your girlfriend. Ask them what they think about the entire situation and get their input. You want to know how they feel about your girlfriend, and how they feel about you dating. Many parents let their children choose if they can have a relationship again. You should never "ask" permission from your children to date. If you do this, your children will begin to think they have the power to deny you relationships; if they want all

your attention, you may not have any relationships until they are in college.

WHAT TO SAY TO YOUR GIRLFRIEND

Your girlfriend will also be going through a lot of emotions when you introduce her to your children. It is important you talk to her and spell things out clearly so she does not assume something that could end the relationship.

1. Explain to your girlfriend that you do not expect her to take on the role of a mother with your children. Tell her all that you ask is that she treats your children with respect.

2. Do not force her to develop a relationship with your children. Instead, give her time to do so on her own. This will allow her to fill a role that the children may be looking for, and it will help both your children and your girlfriend have a better relationship.

3. Your girlfriend probably wants your children to like her, so tell her how she is doing with them. Give her some pointers if she has not been around children much and tell her she is doing a great job. This will help her become more comfortable around the children.

4. Ask your girlfriend to talk to you about her feelings, and what she may be thinking about the children and the relationship in general. Communication is important in any relationship, so it is essential to have it in your new relationship.

You need to look at things from your girlfriend's point of view. She may really care for you, but may not want to be a stepmother. If this is the case, this may not be the relationship for you. While you deserve to be happy, you should not sacrifice your children for that kind of relationship.

Your girlfriend may even resent your children on a subconscious level. If your children take up a lot of your time, she may feel like she is competing with them for your attention. Your girlfriend will also try to determine where she is with your children and how she fits in. Is she a mother figure? Is she a friend? Is she more like a caregiver? This is why it is important to talk to your children and girlfriend so these situations can be avoided. Knowing the roles in a relationship is necessary for its success.

CHAPTER CONCLUSION

One of the hardest things to do after you have lost your wife through divorce or death is to begin dating again. It can be hard to get back into the saddle, but it is important that you do if that is what you want. You deserve happiness and to have someone in your life beyond your children. When your children leave home, what will you have? Should you wait to meet someone until you are in your 50s?

It can be a tricky to start dating again after you have been hurt in a divorce or lost someone as a result of death. You may worry that the same thing will happen again, and you do not want to be hurt again. There is no way to say it will not happen again because it could. The important thing is that you try and get back into the dating game when you feel you are ready. Once you get back into dating, you will feel happier and will regain any confidence you may have lost. While it may take a few tries to find Mrs. Right again, you still can.

There is no reason why you cannot live a long and happy life with a new woman that your children adore and who you love dearly.

You may have fallen in the dirt and been stomped on, but it is time to pick yourself up, dust yourself off, and get ready to face the world again.

Conclusion

Being a father is a full-time job — one that you have for life. No matter how old your children get, you will always be a father and be there for them. They may get older, they may go off for lives of their own and become parents themselves, but that means you are still a father.

A father is a special sort of person. As a father, you are there to help guide your children through life. As a single father, especially if you are widowed, you are often the only parental influence on your children. The actions you take with your children will influence them in adulthood. They will emulate the type of person you are and they will follow your actions. If you are a good person around them, they will grow up with those same morals. If you are a bad person who is mean to others, they will begin to emulate that behavior.

As a single father, you will endure trials that non-single fathers do not go through, but you will also enjoy things that they do not. While you may have to explain to your children about the death of their mother and grieve with them, you will also be the most important person in their lives. If you go through a divorce, your time with your children will be lessened, but you will enjoy the time you have with your children that much more.

As a father, it can sometimes seem like an uphill battle to be able to see your children, let alone get custody of them. It can be difficult to fight in the court for what you see as your right to be with your children. However, that struggle will make you stronger, and will show your children that you are prepared to fight for them.

Being a single father means being something special to your children. You assume all the roles of being a father with your children. You are their teacher, friend, cook, police officer, and best friend. You are there to listen to them, help them, and guide them.

There are going to be tough times, as well as happy times, but through it all you will be proud to say that you were a single father and you did the best job you could to raise the children that you love.

Author Biography

Craig spends most of his time with his wife and their dog, Niko; writing from home; and enjoying what nature provides around his home in Alberta. When he finds the time, he enjoys going to Jasper to hike the mountains.

"Boy, n.: a noise with dirt on it."

— Not Your Average Dictionary

Appendix A

WORK PROPOSAL

Date:

Dear <name of boss>

I, <your name> would like to submit a request to telecommute for my job as <job title> beginning on <date>. As you know, I have recently <been through a divorce/lost my wife> and am juggling home life and work life as a single father. In an effort to balance both, I have come across the solution of telecommuting.

I have done extensive research into this and believe that the impact of telecommuting on my department will include the following:

- <list the impact on your job, the advantages and disadvantages>

Through telecommuting, I will work the same hours I do at the office, but in a more flexible manner so I can juggle being a single father, as well. The area where I will be working in my home will be <describe where you will be working in your home, citing the advantages, including its quiet atmosphere>.

In order to telecommute, I will need the following equipment:

- <list the equipment you will need, if any>

As this would be a significant change to my working arrangement, I would like to speak with you in person so we can determine what I will need from the department and from you, as well as what commitments you will need from me.

If approved, I would like to review my telecommuting agreement in <number of months> months to determine how effective it is with my job performance.

I would like to thank you for your consideration of this proposal.

Sincerely,

Appendix B

QUICK AND HEALTHY MEAL RECIPES FOR THE KIDS

Mushroom-Courgette Burgers

- 4 oz mushrooms, finely chopped
- 1 small onion, chopped
- 1 small courgette, chopped
- 1 carrot, chopped
- 1 oz unsalted peanuts
- 2 cups breadcrumbs
- 2 Tbsp chopped fresh parsley
- 1 tsp yeast extract
- Salt and pepper to taste
- 1 cup uncooked oatmeal, for shaping

Mushroom-Courgette Burgers

Instructions

1. Place the mushrooms in a non-stick pan with a light layer of cooking spray; cook on medium heat. Stir every 10 minutes.

2. Chop the onion, courgette, carrot, and nuts. Mix in a blender.

3. Stir in mushrooms, bread crumbs, parsley, yeast extract, and seasoning to taste.

4. Using oatmeal, shape four burgers.

5. Chill in refrigerator for 15 minutes.

6. Cook the burgers in a non-stick frying pan with a small amount of oil on a grill. Leave on for five minutes, then flip; cook for five more minutes.

Spanish-Style Scrambled Eggs

- 1 tsp vegetable oil
- 1 green onion, chopped
- 1 small ripe tomato, chopped
- 6 large egg whites
- 1 Tbsp salsa or picante sauce
- Ground black pepper to taste
- 1 Tbsp minced fresh cilantro or parsley
- Cilantro or parsley sprigs
- 1 tomato, cut into wedges

Instructions

1. In non-stick skillet, heat oil over medium heat.

2. Stir together onions, tomato, and sauce in skillet. Stir until onions are soft.

3. Reduce heat to low.

4. In a bowl, combine egg whites, salsa or picante sauce, and pepper.

5. Beat until frothy.

6. Add to the skillet.

Spanish-Style Scrambled Eggs

7.   Cook over low heat and stir until it is almost set.

8.   Add cilantro or parsley and stir until eggs are fully set.

9.   Garnish with cilantro or parsley and tomato.

Beef and Mozzarella Cheese

- 1 lb lean ground beef
- 4 cups cooked medium shell macaroni (whole wheat)
- 1 can condensed Italian tomato soup, undiluted
- 1 can condensed cream of mushroom soup, undiluted
- 1¼ cups water
- 1½ cups (6 oz) shredded mozzarella cheese, divided
- 1 tsp dried basil
- ½ tsp pepper
- ⅛ tsp garlic powder or 1 garlic clove, minced

Beef and Mozzarella Cheese

Instructions

1. In a medium skillet over medium to high heat, cook the beef until browned.

2. Drain the grease.

3. Add macaroni, soups, water, 1 cup of cheese, basil, pepper, and garlic powder.

4. Spoon into a 2-quart shallow baking dish.

5. Bake at 400 degree Fahrenheit for 20 minutes. Stir.

6. Sprinkle the remaining shredded cheese over beef and macaroni mixture.

7. Bake five more minutes, or until cheese is melted.

Cheese Stuffed Chicken Breasts

- 1½ cups reduced-fat cream cheese
- ⅔ cup reduced-fat cheddar cheese
- 8 Tbsp butter, divided
- 1 tsp nutmeg
- 3 cups grated Swiss cheese
- 6 skinned and boneless chicken breasts
- ⅓ cup flour
- 2 eggs, beaten
- 1 cup bread crumbs

Instructions

1. Preheat oven to 400 degrees Fahrenheit.

2. Prepare three bowls for rolling the chicken: one with flour, one with eggs, and one with bread crumbs. Set aside.

3. Blend cream cheese, cheddar cheese, 5 tablespoons butter, and nutmeg in a mixing bowl. Allow this mixture to chill for one hour.

4. Cut a slit lengthwise in each chicken breast to form a pocket. Carefully insert cheese and butter mixture into each pocket.

Cheese Stuffed Chicken Breasts

5. Roll each breast in the bowl of flour, then egg, then crumbs and chill one hour again.

6. In an oven-proof skillet, sear breasts in three tablespoons butter over high heat for two to three minutes, or until lightly browned.

7. Transfer pan to preheated oven and bake for seven minutes, or until chicken is thoroughly cooked.

Baked Macaroni with Chicken and Cheese

- 8 oz macaroni, cooked
- 1 rotisserie roasted chicken
- 1 cup prepared alfredo sauce
- 1 cup shredded Monterey Jack cheese
- ½ cup grated Parmesan cheese

Instructions

1. Preheat oven to 350 degrees Fahrenheit.

2. Cook macaroni according to package directions; drain.

Baked Macaroni
with Chicken and Cheese

3. Meanwhile, remove meat from chicken. Discard skin and bones.

4. Cut chicken into one-inch pieces and set aside.

5. In a large bowl, combine macaroni, chicken, alfredo sauce, and Monterey Jack cheese.

6. Mix well and transfer to a 2-quart baking dish.

7. Top with Parmesan cheese and bake until bubbly and lightly browned on top, about 20 minutes.

8. Serve warm.

Ham Salad Wrap

- 1 (8 oz) package reduced-fat cream cheese, softened
- ⅓ cup whipped salad dressing, preferably Miracle Whip
- 3 Tbsp honey
- 1½ cups frozen corn, thawed
- 2 (4½ oz) cans deviled ham spread
- 6 medium-sized corn tortillas
- 2 Tbsp margarine, softened

Instructions

1. Beat cream cheese with salad dressing in a bowl.

2. Once smooth, beat in mustard and honey.

3. Stir in corn and ham.

4. On the tortilla, put softened butter and spread ham mixture over it.

5. Roll and cut in half.

6. Serve and enjoy.

BBQ Chicken

- 1 tsp olive oil
- 3 lbs chicken pieces
- Black pepper
- 16 oz barbecue sauce
- 16 oz of orange soda

Instructions

1. Add olive oil to frying pan over medium heat.

2. Season the chicken on both sides with salt and pepper. When frying pan is hot, put chicken in. Brown on one side, then flip.

3. Add barbeque sauce and orange soda.

4. Cook for about 15 minutes.

Taco Salad

- 1 lb lean ground beef
- 12-oz package of taco seasoning
- 14 oz can black beans (drained)
- 1 cup sour cream
- 1 cup salsa
- 14½ oz bag tortilla chips
- 10 oz bag lettuce
- ¼ cup chopped red onion
- 1 cup shredded cheddar cheese
- ¼ cup chopped cilantro

Instructions

1. In a large skillet, cook the ground beef and drain. Put the beef back in the skillet.

2. Add in taco seasoning.

3. Stir in black beans and set aside.

4. Mix sour cream and salsa together and set aside.

5. Put chips on bottom of a serving bowl.

6. Add lettuce to the top of the bowl.

Taco Salad

7. Put ground beef on top of the lettuce.

8. Put sour cream-salsa dressing over the top and add in the cheese and cilantro with onion.

Chicken Stir-Fry

- 1 lb of boneless, skinless chicken breast (cut into one-inch chunks)
- ⅓ cup cornstarch
- ¼ cup soy sauce
- ½ cup orange marmalade
- 1 Tbsp minced garlic
- 1 tsp minced ginger
- ¼ tsp red pepper flakes
- Salt and pepper
- 2 tsp canola oil

Chicken Stir-Fry

Instructions

1. Put chicken breast pieces in a large zipped plastic bag.

2. Put cornstarch in bag and toss to coat.

3. Whisk together soy sauce, marmalade, garlic, ginger, and red pepper in a bowl. Add salt and pepper.

4. Heat wok over high heat.

5. Add in canola oil.

6. Add in chicken.

7. Cook chicken until no longer pink.

8. Pour sauce over chicken and cook further until chicken is coated.

Serving suggestion: Serve with rice.

Crock Pot Chili

- 1 lb ground beef
- 1 yellow onion (diced)
- 1 green pepper (diced)
- 2 Tbsp chili powder
- 1 Tbsp minced garlic
- 1 Tbsp ground cumin
- 1 12 oz can diced tomatoes
- 1 14 oz can black beans (drained)
- 1 14 oz can chili beans (undrained)
- ½ cup ketchup
- Salt and pepper
- ¼ cup shredded cheddar cheese
- ¼ cup sour cream

Instructions

1. Cook ground beef in large skillet.
2. Drain beef and put in slow cooker.
3. Add rest of ingredients to ketchup.
4. Cook on high for four to five hours (or low heat for six to eight hours).
5. Before serving, add salt and pepper.
6. Garnish with cheese and sour cream.

"There are no seven wonders of the world in the eyes of a child. There are seven million."

— Walt Streightiff, Author

Bibliography

Books

Brentano, Cornelia and Clark-Stewart Alison, *Divorce: Causes and Consequences*, Yale University Press, 2006.

Brott, Armin, *The Single Father: A Dad's Guide To Parenting Without A Partner*, Abbeville Press, 1999.

James, Kevin, *Surviving The Single Dad Syndrome*, Publish America, 2004.

Mandelstein, Paul, *Always Dad, Being A Great Father During and After Divorce*, Nolo Publishing, 2006.

Shimberg, Elaine and Michael, *The Complete Single Father*, Adams Media, 2007.

Klumpp, Mike, *The Single Dad's Survival Book*, WaterBrook Press, 2003.

Web sites

Center for Children's Justice, Inc. (**www.childrensjustice.org/**)

Divorce Lawyer Source (**www.divorce-lawyer-source.com/**)

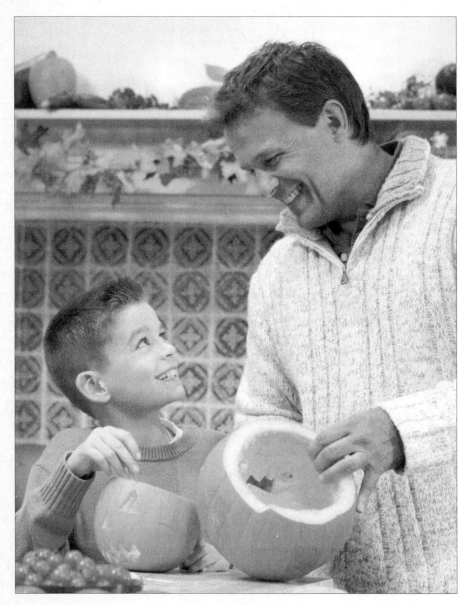

Index

N

Nanny, 127-128, 136-139, 141-144, 146-147

Negative thinking, 172-173

No-Fault Divorce, 40, 42-43

P

Pink eye, 187-188

Positive Role Model, 294

Primary residential custody, 32

Puberty, 214, 255-256, 258-262, 271, 276-277, 281, 283-285, 287, 295, 14-15, 21

R

Reye's syndrome, 197

Roseola, 188, 200

Rotating custody, 33

S

Serial custody, 35

Sick days, 117-118

Signs of Stress, 61, 65

Sole parental responsibility, 32

Solo sports, 265

Split custody, 34

Sportsmanship, 266-268

Summary Divorce, 41

T

Team sports, 265

Telecommuting, 313-314, 111

Third-party custody, 35

Tonsillitis, 189-190

U

Uncontested Divorce, 41

Urinary tract infection, 190-191

V

Video game systems, 238, 268